LAWS AND LEGISLATION

JUDGE SONIA SOTOMAYOR:

SELECTED OPTIONS

LAWS AND LEGISLATION

Clean Diamond Trade Act
James T. Williams
(Editor)
2009. ISBN: 978-1-60741-111-6

Revisiting and Evaluating the Congressional Review Act
Katherine R. Williamson
(Editor)
2009. ISBN: 978-1-60692-687-1

State Secrets Protection Act
Lara H. Nellington
(Editor)
2009. ISBN: 978-1-60692-711-3

Restoring the Rule of Law
Patricia V. Barkley
(Editor)
2009. ISBN: 978-1-60692-970-4

Federal Torts Reform, Claims and Liability
Ben V. Colligan
(Editor)
2009. ISBN: 978-1-60692-989-6

Contemporary Perspectives on Legal Regulation of Sexual Behavior: Psycho-legal Research and Analysis
Monica K. Miller
(Editor)
2009. ISBN: 978-1-60741-161-1 (Hardcover)

Contemporary Perspectives on Legal Regulation of Sexual Behavior: Psycho-legal Research and Analysis
Monica K. Miller
(Editor)
2009. ISBN: 978-1-60876-779-3 (E-book))

Abortion: Legislative and Legal Issues
Kevin G. Nolan
(Editor)
2010. ISBN: 978-1-60741-522-0

Copyright Law and A Brief Look at the Google Library Project
Brett D. Rhodes
(Editor)
2010. ISBN: 978-1-60741-871-9

A Comparative Analysis of Disability Laws
John R. Vaughn
2010. ISBN: 978-1-60741-536-7

Antitrust Modernization
Luigi Ferrigno
(Editor)
2010. ISBN: 978-1-60741-805-4

Copyright and the Orphan Works Issue
Andrew D. Owens
(Editor)
2010. ISBN: 978-1-60741-721-7

How Laws are Made in the U.S.A.
Helen Maes
(Editor)
2010. ISBN: 978-1-60876-142-5

Judge Sonia Sotomayor: Selected Options
Patrick K. Reed (Editor)
2010. ISBN: 978-1-60876-759-5

The laws of Science and the Science of Law, Case Studies in Expert Testimony on Chemistry
Hyman Davidson Gesser, A.B. Bass and Bradley Myers
2010. ISBN: 978-1-60876-807-3

How Pretrial Publicity Affects Juror Decision Making and Memory
Christine L. Ruva
2010. ISBN: 978-1-61668-328-3 (Softcover)
How Pretrial Publicity Affects Juror Decision Making and Memory
Christine L. Ruva
2010. ISBN: 978-1-61668-587-4 (E-book))

American Recovery and Reinvestment Act: History, Overview, Impact
Paul G. Tellis (Editor)
2010. ISBN: 978-1-61668-355-9 (Hardcover)

American Recovery and Reinvestment Act: History, Overview, Impact
Paul G. Tellis (Editor)
2010. ISBN: 978-1-61668-390-0 (E-book))

Congressional Compromise: Amendments between the House and the Senate
Julio D. Nachtrieb and Liam J. Cadriel (Editors)
2010. ISBN: 978-1-60741-796-5 (Hardcover)

Congressional Compromise: Amendments between the House and the Senate
Julio D. Nachtrieb and Liam J. Cadriel (Editors)
2010. ISBN: 978-1-61668-884-4 (E-book))

LAWS AND LEGISLATION

JUDGE SONIA SOTOMAYOR:

SELECTED OPTIONS

PATRICK K. REED
EDITOR

Nova Science Publishers, Inc.
New York

For permission to use material from this book please contact us:
Telephone 631-231-7269; Fax 631-231-8175
Web Site: http://www.novapublishers.com

LIBRARY OF CONGRESS CATALOGING-IN-PUBLICATION DATA

Judge Sonia Sotomayor : selected options / editor, Patrick K. Reed.
p. cm.
CRS report for Congress.
Includes bibliographical references and index.
ISBN 978-1-60876-759-5 (softcover : alk. paper)
1. Judicial opinions--United States 2. Sotomayor, Sonia, 1954- 3. People with disabilities--Legal status, laws, etc.--United States. 4. Human reproduction--Law and legislation--United States. I. Reed, Patrick K. II. Library of Congress. Congressional Research Service.
KF213.S665R44 2010
347.73'2634--dc22
[B]

2009045949

Published by Nova Science Publishers, Inc. ✢ New York

CONTENTS

Preface		**ix**
Chapter 1	Civil Rights of Individuals with Disabilities: The Opinions of Judge Sotomayor *Nancy Lee Jones and Carol J. Toland*	**1**
Chapter 2	Judge Sonia Sotomayor: Analysis of Selected Opinions *Anna C. Henning and Kenneth R. Thomas*	**19**
Chapter 3	The Nomination of Judge Sonia Sotomayor: A Review of Second Circuit Decisions Relating to Reproductive Rights *Jon O. Shimabukuro*	**93**
Chapter Sources		**103**
Index		**105**

PREFACE

Judge Sonia Sotomayor was nominated by President Obama to the U.S. Supreme Court on May 26, 2009. This book explores and examines selected opinions written by Judge Sotomayor relating to the civil rights of individuals with disabilities and includes a discussion of cases relating to the Americans with Disabilities Act (ADA), and also reviews her opinions involving abortion and family planning practices. This book considers also Judge Sotomayor's extensive record, compiled from years as a lawyer, prosecutor, district court judge, and appellate court judge, to better understand her legal approaches and judicial philosophy. This book consists of public documents which have been located, gathered, combined, reformatted, and enhanced with a subject index, selectively edited and bound to provide easy access.

Chapter 1 - Judge Sonia Sotomayor was nominated by President Obama to the U.S. Supreme Court on May 26, 2009. This report examines selected opinions written by Judge Sotomayor relating to the civil rights of individuals with disabilities and includes a discussion of cases relating to the Americans with Disabilities Act (ADA), Section 504 of the Rehabilitation Act, the Protection and Advocacy for Individuals with Mental Illness Act (PAIMI), and the Individuals with Disabilities Education Act (IDEA). In addition, selected dissents, concurrences, and decisions where Judge Sotomayor joined the majority are examined.

Judge Sotomayor's decisions are generally supportive of individuals with disabilities, but she does not always rule in favor of plaintiffs with disabilities. In her most discussed decision on disability issues, *Bartlett v. New York State Board of Bar Examiners*, she anticipated the legislative discussions surrounding the enactment of the ADA Amendments Act by finding that the use of self accommodations did not mean that the plaintiff was not an individual with a disability. While analyzing the statutory and regulatory language, Judge Sotomayor also examined the implications of various legal arguments noting that if a definition of disability is based on outcomes alone, it would preclude coverage of many individuals who have worked to overcome their disabilities. As is indicated by *Bartlett* and Judge Sotomayor's decisions relating to protection and advocacy agencies, she appears to look at the general purposes of a statute when interpreting its specific provisions.

Judge Sotomayor's decisions often turn on the particular facts presented. Judge Sotomayor also examines the statutory language at issue, as well as the applicable regulations and guidance to inform her decisions. She also has relied upon the reasoning of other circuits in arriving at her decisions.

Chapter 2 - In May 2009, Supreme Court Justice David Souter announced his intention to retire from the Supreme Court. Several weeks later, President Obama nominated Judge Sonia Sotomayor, who currently serves on the U.S. Court of Appeals for the Second Circuit, to fill his seat. To fulfill its constitutional "advice and consent" function, the Senate will consider Judge Sotomayor's extensive record – compiled from years as a lawyer, prosecutor, district court judge, and appellate court judge – to better understand her legal approaches and judicial philosophy.

This report provides an analysis of selected opinions authored by Judge Sotomayor during her tenure as a judge on the Second Circuit. Discussions of the selected opinions are grouped according to various topics of legal significance.

As a group, the opinions belie easy categorization along any ideological spectrum. However, it is possible to draw some conclusions regarding Judge Sotomayor's judicial approach, both within some specific issue areas and in general.

Perhaps the most consistent characteristic of Judge Sotomayor 's approach as an appellate judge has been an adherence to the doctrine of *stare decisis*, i.e., the upholding of past judicial precedents. Other characteristics appear to include what many would describe as a careful application of particular facts at issue in a case and a dislike for situations in which the court might be seen as oversteping its judicial role.

It is difficult to determine the extent to which Judge Sotomayor 's style as a judge on the Second Circuit would predict her style should she become a Supreme Court justice. However, as has been the case historically with other nominees, some of her approaches may be enduring characteristics.

Chapter 3 - On May 26, 2009, Judge Sonia Sotomayor of the U.S. Court of Appeals for the Second Circuit was nominated to replace retiring U.S. Supreme Court Justice David H. Souter. During her tenure with the Second Circuit, Judge

Sotomayor has not addressed substantive legal questions involving abortion, such as the extent of the Constitution's protection of a woman's right to choose. Judge Sotomayor has, however, authored opinions that have considered the impact of foreign funding restrictions on domestic nonprofit organizations that promote abortion, discussed the effect of forced abortions and involuntary family planning practices in the context of applications for asylum, and examined possible municipal liability resulting from anti-abortion demonstrations. This report reviews Judge Sotomayor's opinions involving abortion and family planning practices.

On May 26, 2009, Judge Sonia Sotomayor of the U.S. Court of Appeals for the Second Circuit was nominated to replace retiring U.S. Supreme Court Justice David H. Souter. During her tenure with the Second Circuit, Judge Sotomayor has not addressed substantive legal questions involving abortion, such as the extent of the Constitution's protection of a woman's right to choose. Judge Sotomayor has, however, authored opinions that have considered the impact of foreign funding restrictions on domestic nonprofit organizations that promote abortion, discussed the effect of forced abortions and involuntary family planning practices in the context of applications for asylum, and examined possible municipal liability resulting from anti-abortion demonstrations.

This report reviews Judge Sotomayor's opinions involving abortion and family planning practices. Some have questioned Judge Sotomayor's position on abortion, particularly in light of her affiliation with the Puerto Rican Legal Defense and Education Fund, which joined other advocacy organizations in promoting abortion rights in amicus briefs filed with the Court between 1980 and 1992. A review of Judge Sotomayor 's opinions on abortion and family planning, however, suggests a respect for precedent and an adherence to established legal standards.

In: Judge Sonia Sotomayor: Selected Options
Editors: Patrick K. Reed
ISBN: 978-1-60876-759-5

Chapter 1

CIVIL RIGHTS OF INDIVIDUALS WITH DISABILITIES: THE OPINIONS OF JUDGE SOTOMAYOR

Nancy Lee Jones and Carol J. Toland

SUMMARY

Judge Sonia Sotomayor was nominated by President Obama to the U.S. Supreme Court on May 26, 2009. This report examines selected opinions written by Judge Sotomayor relating to the civil rights of individuals with disabilities and includes a discussion of cases relating to the Americans with Disabilities Act (ADA), Section 504 of the Rehabilitation Act, the Protection and Advocacy for Individuals with Mental Illness Act (PAIMI), and the Individuals with Disabilities Education Act (IDEA). In addition, selected dissents, concurrences, and decisions where Judge Sotomayor joined the majority are examined.

Judge Sotomayor's decisions are generally supportive of individuals with disabilities, but she does not always rule in favor of plaintiffs with disabilities. In her most discussed decision on disability issues, *Bartlett v. New York State Board of Bar Examiners*, she anticipated the legislative discussions surrounding the enactment of the ADA Amendments Act by finding that the use of self accommodations did not mean that the plaintiff was not an individual with a disability. While analyzing the statutory and regulatory language, Judge

Sotomayor also examined the implications of various legal arguments noting that if a definition of disability is based on outcomes alone, it would preclude coverage of many individuals who have worked to overcome their disabilities. As is indicated by *Bartlett* and Judge Sotomayor's decisions relating to protection and advocacy agencies, she appears to look at the general purposes of a statute when interpreting its specific provisions.

Judge Sotomayor's decisions often turn on the particular facts presented. Judge Sotomayor also examines the statutory language at issue, as well as the applicable regulations and guidance to inform her decisions. She also has relied upon the reasoning of other circuits in arriving at her decisions.

INTRODUCTION

Judge Sonia Sotomayor was nominated by President Obama to the U.S. Supreme Court on May 26, 2009. This report examines selected opinions written by Judge Sotomayor relating to the civil rights of individuals with disabilities and includes a discussion of cases relating to the Americans with Disabilities Act (ADA),[1] Section 504 of the Rehabilitation Act,[2] the Protection and Advocacy for Individuals with Mental Illness Act (PAIMI),[3] and the Individuals with Disabilities Education Act (IDEA).[4] In addition, selected dissents, concurrences, and decisions where Judge Sotomayor joined the majority are examined.

Judge Sotomayor's decisions are generally supportive of individuals with disabilities, but she does not always rule in favor of plaintiffs with disabilities. In her most discussed decision on disability issues, *Bartlett v. New York State Board of Bar Examiners*,[5] she anticipated the legislative discussions surrounding the enactment of the ADA Amendments Act by finding that the use of self accommodations did not mean that the plaintiff was not an individual with a disability.[6] While analyzing the statutory and regulatory language, Judge Sotomayor also examined the implications of various legal arguments noting that if a definition of disability is based on outcomes alone, it would preclude coverage of many individuals who have worked to overcome their disabilities. As is indicated by *Bartlett* and Judge Sotomayor's decisions relating to protection and advocacy agencies,[7] she appears to look at the general purposes of a statute when interpreting its specific provisions.

Judge Sotomayor's decisions often turn on the particular facts presented. For example, in *Pell v. Columbia University*,[8] the specific facts surrounding the allegations of hostility to the plaintiff's dyslexia and the alleged discrimination regarding a foreign language requirement were closely examined.[9] Analysis of other decisions shows Judge Sotomayor also examines the statutory language at issue,[10] as well as the applicable regulations and guidance[11] to inform her decisions. She also has relied upon the reasoning of other circuits in arriving at her decisions.[12]

THE AMERICANS WITH DISABILITIES ACT (ADA)

Overview

The Americans with Disabilities Act (ADA)[13] is a broad civil rights act prohibiting discrimination against individuals with disabilities. As stated in the act, its purpose is "to provide a clear and comprehensive national mandate for the elimination of discrimination against individuals with disabilities."[14] The ADA provides broad nondiscrimination protection for individuals with disabilities and is divided into five titles: employment (Title I); public services (Title II); public accommodation and services operated by private entities (Title III); telecommunications (Title IV); and miscellaneous provisions (Title V). While serving on the Second Circuit and the district court, Judge Sotomayor has written, joined in, and dissented in several ADA decisions.

Decisions on the Definition of Disability

Statutory Definition

The threshold issue in any ADA case is whether the individual alleging discrimination is an individual with a disability. Several Supreme Court decisions have interpreted the definition of disability, generally limiting its application.[15] After these Supreme Court interpretations, lower court decisions also interpreted the definition of disability strictly. Congress responded to these decisions by enacting the ADA Amendments Act, P.L. 110-325, which rejects the Supreme Court and lower court interpretations and amends the ADA to provide broader coverage.[16] Two of the major changes made by the ADA Amendments Act are to expand the current interpretation of when an impairment substantially limits a major life activity (rejecting the Supreme Court's interpretation in *Toyota*), and to require that the determination of whether an impairment substantially limits a major life activity must be made without regard to the use of mitigating measures (rejecting the Supreme Court's decisions in *Sutton*, *Murphy*, and *Kirkingburg*).

The ADA Amendments Act defines the term disability with respect to an individual as "(A) a physical or mental impairment that substantially limits one or more of the major life activities of such individual; (B) a record of such an impairment; or (C) being regarded as having such an impairment (as described in paragraph (3))."[17] Although this is essentially the same statutory language as was in the original ADA, P.L. 110-325 contains new rules of construction regarding the definition of disability, which provide that

- the definition of disability shall be construed in favor of broad coverage to the maximum extent permitted by the terms of the act;
- the term "substantially limits" shall be interpreted consistently with the findings and purposes of the ADA Amendments Act;
- an impairment that substantially limits one major life activity need not limit other major life activities to be considered a disability;
- an impairment that is episodic or in remission is a disability if it would have substantially limited a major life activity when active; and
- the determination of whether an impairment substantially limits a major life activity shall be made without regard to the ameliorative effects of mitigating measures, except that the ameliorative effects of ordinary eyeglasses or contact lenses shall be considered.[18]

Judge Sotomayor's Decisions and Dissent

Judge Sotomayor's opinions on the definition of disability all predate the ADA Amendments Act. Although her last opinion in the *Bartlett v. New York State Board of Law Examiners*[19] series of decisions foreshadows some of the rationale for the ADA Amendments Act, much of her reasoning in *Bartlett* and other ADA decisions are based on specific factual issues, regulatory interpretations, and case law.

Bartlett v. New York State Board of Law Examiners[20] is Judge Sotomayor's most discussed decision on disability issues. Essentially, Judge Sotomayor held that a law school graduate with a learning disability was an individual with a disability and, under the ADA, was entitled to accommodations, including extra time, while taking the bar examination.

The procedural history of this case is complicated. In her initial decision at the district court level, Judge Sotomayor held that the plaintiff was an individual with a disability under both the ADA and Section 504, although when compared to the average person in the general population, the plaintiff was found not to be substantially limited in the major life activity of reading due to her self accommodations. However, Judge Sotomayor found that taking the bar exam "implicates the major life activity of working" and that when the plaintiff's reading skills were compared with individuals with comparable training, her reading skills were considerably below normal and, therefore, she was entitled to reasonable accommodations.[21] On appeal, the Second Circuit agreed that the plaintiff was an individual with a disability but on different grounds. The Second Circuit rejected the consideration of the plaintiff's ability to self accommodation and found that she was limited in the major life activity of reading.[22] The Supreme Court then granted *certiorari* and vacated and remanded the Second Circuit's decision[23] for reconsideration in light of the Supreme Court's decision in *Sutton v. United Air Lines*,[24] *Murphy v. United Parcel Service*,[25] and *Albertsons v. Kirkingburg.*[26] These decisions, as noted above, limited the definition of disability by holding that corrective devices and mitigating measures must be considered in determining whether an individual is an individual with a disability and were specifically rejected by Congress in the enactment of the ADA Amendments Act. On remand from the Supreme Court, the Second Circuit remanded the decision to the district court to consider whether the plaintiff's reading ability was substantially limited by any measure and whether the plaintiff was substantially limited in the major life activity of working.[27]

Bartlett's long procedural journey finally ended when Judge Sotomayor held a four-day remand trial with testimony by numerous experts and witnesses.[28] Judge Sotomayor, guided by the Supreme Court's decisions and factual testimony, held that the plaintiff was substantially limited in the major life activity of reading and, in the alternative, substantially limited in the major life activity of working. Although Judge Sotomayor noted that the plaintiff used certain self accommodations or coping strategies, she found that these "merely help plaintiff function, but do not affect her ability to read" and, therefore, were not relevant in a determination of whether the plaintiff has a reading disability. Judge Sotomayor, anticipating the legislative discussions surrounding the enactment of the ADA Amendments Act, stated the following:

> A definition of disability based on outcomes alone, particularly in the context of learning disabilities, would prevent a court from finding a disability in

the case of any individual like Dr. Bartlett who is extremely bright and hardworking, and who uses alternative routes to achieve academic success.[29]

Judge Sotomayor's decisions in *Bartlett* both anticipated the Supreme Court's denial of the use of mitigating measures and anticipated Congress's rejection of the Supreme Court's interpretation. In the first *Bartlett* case, Judge Sotomayor held that the plaintiff was an individual with a disability, but did so by finding that she was substantially limited in the major life activity of working. Judge Sotomayor found that the plaintiff was not substantially limited in the activity of reading since her self accommodations enabled her to read. This use of the mitigating measure of the plaintiff's self accommodation pre-shadowed the Supreme Court's interpretation of the definition of disability which found that the decision on whether an individual has a disability is made with the use of whatever mitigating measure the individual employed. Specifically, the Supreme Court in *Albertsons v. Kirkingburg*[30] held that a trucker with monocular vision who was able to compensate for this impairment was not a person with a disability. However, Judge Sotomayor arrived at her interpretation by reliance on ADA regulations interpreting the term "substantially limited," a regulatory interpretation which was rejected by the ADA Amendments Act.[31] The Second Circuit, after the case was remanded from the Supreme Court, found that Judge Sotomayor had properly considered the plaintiff's self accommodations but found that Judge Sotomayor's findings that the plaintiff had average skills on some measures of reading was insufficient to conclude that the plaintiff was not substantially limited in reading. When Judge Sotomayor considered *Bartlett* on remand, she addressed the Second Circuit's comments and, after examining additional evidence, concluded that the plaintiff was substantially limited in the major life activity of reading. And, as noted above, Judge Sotomayor anticipated some of the legislative discussions surrounding the enactment of the ADA Amendments Act regarding a "catch 22" situation by finding that the use of self accommodations did not mean that the plaintiff was not an individual with a disability.[32]

The third prong of the definition of disability, being regarded as having a disability, was at issue in *Equal Employment Opportunity Commission v. J.B. Hunt Transport, Inc.*[33] The majority in *Hunt* found no violation of the ADA and held that the employer had not perceived the applicants to have a disability. The majority reasoned that the alleged inability to drive a truck due to the use of certain medications did not constitute a substantial limitation on working and, therefore, the plaintiffs were not regarded as having a disability. Judge Sotomayor wrote a strong dissent, disagreeing with the majority's factual determinations and finding that the Equal Employment Opportunity Commission (EEOC) had provided substantial evidence that the employer had believed that the plaintiffs were unfit to drive a truck and not merely "unsuited for long-distance driving in Hunt's 40-ton trucks.... "[34]

Title I—Employment

Statutory Provisions

Title I of the ADA provides that no covered entity shall discriminate against a qualified individual on the basis of disability in regard to job application procedures; the hiring, advancement, or discharge of employees; employee compensation; job training; and other terms, conditions, and privileges of employment.[35] The term employer is defined as a person engaged in an industry affecting commerce who has 15 or more employees.[36] If the issue raised under the ADA is employment related, and the threshold issues of meeting the definition of an individual with a disability and involving an employer employing over 15 individuals are met, the next step is to determine whether the individual is a qualified individual with a disability who, with or without reasonable accommodation, can perform the essential functions of the job.

Decisions Written by Judge Sotomayor

Judge Sotomayor's decisions have not always found for an individual with a disability. Whether an individual is a qualified individual with a disability was at issue in *Valentine v. Standard & Poor's.*[37] The plaintiff, an analyst at Standard & Poors, had been diagnosed with bipolar disorder. His job performance had deteriorated and after he left "an obnoxious and taunting" voice mail message for a co-worker, his employment was terminated. Judge Sotomayor found no discrimination under the ADA stating that "the ADA does not protect disabled employees from all adverse employment decisions."[38] Whether or not the misconduct was a manifestation of a disability was seen as irrelevant since "the ADA does not immunize disabled employees from discipline or discharge for incidents of misconduct in the workplace."[39]

An employer's responsibilities regarding reasonable accommodations for an employee was at issue in *Parker v. Columbia Pictures Industries.*[40] In *Parker* the employee sustained a back injury at work, had back surgery, and used six months of paid short-term disability leave. After the disability leave was exhausted, the employee contacted the employer about part-time work. The employer terminated the employment and advised the employee about long-term disability benefits, and the employee applied for the long-term disability benefits and Social Security disability benefits. The Second Circuit, in an opinion by Judge Sotomayor, vacated the district court's grant of summary judgment for the employer and remanded the case for a determination of whether there was a triable question of fact. Judge Sotomayor observed the following:

> The duty to make reasonable accommodations does not, of course, require an employer to hold an injured employee's position open indefinitely while the employee attempts to recover, nor does it force an employer to investigate every aspect of an employee's condition before terminating him based on his inability to work. At the very least, however, an employee who proposed an accommodation while still on short-term leave—as Parker did here, at least two weeks prior to his termination—triggers a responsibility on the employer's part to investigate that request and determine its feasibility.[41]

Judge Sotomayor also addressed the issue of liability for mixed-motive actions in *Parker.* Following decisions in other circuits that applied the liability for mixed-motive actions used under Title VII of the Civil Rights Act[42] to the ADA, Judge Sotomayor applied Title VII's mixed motive analysis to the ADA.

In the earlier case of *Norville v. Staten Island University Hospital,*[43] Judge Sotomayor also examined the issue of reasonable accommodation in an employment discrimination context. *Norville* involved a nurse who suffered a spinal injury on the job, was on an extended leave of absence, and then sought to return to work. Her previous job was no longer available, and the hospital offered her part-time work or full-time work at another site. Both of these offers would have had adverse effects on her pension. The plaintiff then applied for a full-time position but another candidate was hired. Judge Sotomayor examined the statutory requirements for reasonable accommodations, which include reassignment to a vacant position; noted the Equal Employment Opportunity Commission (EEOC) guidelines stating that the new position should be equivalent; and concluded that "where a comparable position is vacant and the disabled employee is qualified for the position, an employer's refusal to reassign the employee to that position absent some other offer of reasonable accommodation—constitutes a violation of the ADA."[44] Applying this analysis to *Norville,* Judge Sotomayor found that the trial court instructions to the jury were inadequate since they did not specify that the offer of an inferior position was not a reasonable accommodation when a comparable position is available. The instructions were found to be prejudicial to the plaintiff, and the case was remanded for further proceedings.

In two fact-specific decisions regarding the application of the ADA's statute of limitations, Judge Sotomayor arrived at two different rulings. In *Lloret v. Lockwood Greene Engineers, Inc.*,[45] Judge Sotomayor held that the ADA's statute of limitations for bringing an employment discrimination suit was applicable and that the plaintiff had not presented sufficient evidence regarding a mental disability to warrant the tolling of the statute of limitations. However, in *Brown v. Parkchester South Condominiums*,[46] another case alleging employment discrimination under the ADA, Judge Sotomayor found that there was sufficient documentation to warrant an evidentiary hearing to determine whether the plaintiff's medical conditions warranted tolling the applicable filing deadline.

Title II—Public Services

Title II of the ADA provides that no qualified individual with a disability shall be excluded from participation in or be denied the benefits of the services, programs, or activities of a public entity or be subjected to discrimination by any such entity.[47] "Public entity" is defined as state and local governments, any department or other instrumentality of a state or local government, and certain transportation authorities.

In *Anthony v. City of New York*,[48] police responded to a 911 call and found Myra Anthony, an adult woman with Down Syndrome, alone. Since they were unable to locate her caretaker, the police transported the woman to the psychiatric ward of a hospital where she was detained overnight. Ms. Anthony sued alleging in part a violation of Title II of the ADA. Although Judge Sotomayor noted that there might be a Title II ADA claim if the seizure and hospitalization were motivated by discrimination against individuals with disabilities, she found no evidence of such motivation. The district court's grant of summary judgment for the city on the ADA claim was affirmed.

Judge Sotomayor also found no violation of Title II of the ADA in *Lai v. New York City Government*[49] where she joined in a *per curiam* decision. In *Lai*, the plaintiff argued that a city policy giving special parking privileges to individuals with disabilities who lived, worked, or attended school in the city but did not give the same rights to individuals with out-of-state disabilities permits was violative of the ADA. The *per curiam* decision found that the city's policy "discriminates on the basis of residency and not disability" and, therefore, did not run afoul of Title II of the ADA.

Section 504 of the Rehabilitation Act

Section 504 of the Rehabilitation Act of 1973 prohibits discrimination against an otherwise qualified individual with a disability, solely on the basis of the disability, in any program or activity that receives federal financial assistance, the executive agencies, or the U.S. Postal Service.[50] Many of the concepts used in the ADA originated in Section 504 and its interpretations; however, there is one major difference. While Section 504's prohibition against discrimination is tied to the receipt of federal financial assistance, the ADA also covers entities not receiving such funds. In addition, the federal executive agencies and the U.S. Postal Service are covered under Section 504, not the ADA.

In *Pell v. Columbia University*,[51] Judge Sotomayor examined a claim involving, among other issues, questions about an harassment on the basis of disability claim under Section 504, and about a lack of accommodation regarding a foreign language requirement. Judge Sotomayor held that the allegations of hostility to the plaintiff's dyslexia were "more than adequate to warrant denying Columbia's motion to dismiss." However, Judge Sotomayor granted Columbia University's motion to dismiss regarding the alleged discrimination on the foreign language requirement, finding that the plaintiff failed to make a showing that she was discriminated against since Columbia accepted her transfer credits in French as fulfilling their requirements.

Protection and Advocacy for Individuals with Mental Illness Act (PAIMI)

PAIMI was enacted to ensure that "the rights of individuals with mental illness are protected" and "to assist States to establish and operate a protection and advocacy system for individuals with mental illness."[52] The protection and advocacy systems (P & A's) are to "protect and advocate the rights of such individuals" and "investigate incidents of abuse and neglect."[53] Federal funds are provided to states that meet the requirements of the act,[54] and these requirements include having access to patient records.[55] Judge Sotomayor's decisions have been supportive of the purposes of PAIMI and other federal statutes relating to P & A systems, and her opinions have not supported limitations on their authority to investigate complaints.

In *Protection & Advocacy for Persons with Disabilities v. Mental Health & Addiction Services*,[56] the Connecticut P & A system sued for access to peer review records on two patients who had died while institutionalized. Joining the Third and Tenth Circuits, Judge Sotomayor held the statutory language was clear in its requirement for disclosure of "all records."

Similarly, in *Connecticut Office of Protection and Advocacy for Persons with Disabilities v. Hartford Board of Education,*[57] Judge Sotomayor addressed whether the Connecticut P & A system should have access to a nonresidential school for children with serious emotional disturbances in order to investigate allegations of abuse and neglect. The main issue was whether the nonresidential nature of the program limited the rights of the P & A system to investigate. Finding that the P & A system had such rights, Judge Sotomayor relied upon recent amendments to PAIMI which specifically extended the statute's reach to individuals living in the community. In addition, she found that the Developmental Disabilities Assistance and Bill of Rights Act (DD Act)[58] and the Protection and Advocacy for Individual Rights Act (PAIR)[59] also supported the right of a P & A to have access to the school. In arriving at this holding, Judge Sotomayor examined the purposes of the DD Act to protect the legal and human rights of individuals with developmental disabilities and found that these purposes were not limited by the fact that a section of the DD Act specifically provides authority to investigate certain incidents.

The Individuals with Disabilities Education Act (IDEA)

The Individuals with Disabilities Education Act (IDEA)[60] is both a grants statute and a civil rights statute. It provides federal funding for the education of children with disabilities and requires, as a condition for the receipt of such funds, the provision of a free appropriate public education (FAPE) in the least restrictive environment (LRE). The statute also contains detailed due process provisions to ensure the provision of FAPE. Originally enacted in 1975, the act responded to increased awareness of the need to educate children with disabilities, and to judicial decisions requiring that states provide an education for children with disabilities if they provided an education for children without disabilities.[61] Judge Sotomayor has written several IDEA decisions while serving on the Second Circuit. One commentator found that in decisions involving IDEA before the Second Circuit, Judge Sotomayor ruled in favor of school districts 58% of the time.[62]

Her decisions, as illustrated by *Taylor v. Vermont Department of Education et al.,*[63] rely upon the statute, judicial interpretations, and Department of Education interpretations to inform her reasoning.

In *Taylor v. Vermont Department of Education et al.*,[64] Judge Sotomayor analyzed the rights under IDEA of a natural parent who does not have custody of the child. IDEA states that the term "parent" "*includes* a legal guardian,"[65] and the regulations more comprehensively define the term.[66] In this case, Pam Taylor, the natural mother of L.D., was not awarded any parental rights of L.D. in her final custody arrangement as part of her Vermont divorce decree. Beginning in fall 1998, L.D. was assessed and evaluated multiple times for emotional-behavioral disabilities, and Taylor, claiming a right as a "parent" under IDEA, sought access to records of these evaluations and increased involvement in decisions made about her daughter's special education. Following. several unsuccessful attempts to pursue her rights under IDEA administratively, Taylor filed suit with the district court.[67] The case was dismissed because the court held that Taylor lacked standing as a non-custodial parent, and Taylor appealed the decision. On appeal, Judge Sotomayor, in analyzing IDEA, its respective regulations, and case law, recognized the Department of Education's decision that "the allocation of parental rights under the IDEA is best left to local domestic law."[68] As a result, she analyzed Taylor's rights under the Vermont divorce decree and held that, because Taylor had no "authority to make education decisions on behalf of L.D." in her Vermont divorce decree, Taylor therefore lacked standing to demand a hearing under IDEA.[69] However, Judge Sotomayor found that Taylor could pursue her record-access claim under the IDEA "[b]ecause the custody decree has not 'specifically revoked' her informational access prerogatives."[70]

In *Murphy v. Arlington Central School District Board of Education*,[71] Judge Sotomayor examined a claim involving the "stay put" provision of IDEA.[72] The "stay put" provision guarantees that, during the pendency of administrative proceedings, "unless the State or local educational agency and the parents otherwise agree, the child shall remain in the then-current educational placement of the child.... "[73] In this case, the Murphys, parents of a child with a disability as defined by IDEA, petitioned the district court for an injunction requiring the Arlington school board to pay for their son Joseph's education at a private school while administrative proceedings were pending. The district court held that Joseph's private school was his "current educational placement" and therefore, under IDEA's stay put provision, "Arlington was obligated to pay for Joseph's schooling until such time as Joseph's placement was changed in accordance with the IDEA."[74] On appeal, Judge Sotomayor affirmed the district court's ruling on both procedural and substantive grounds. First, she held that the district court properly exercised jurisdiction over the claim even though the Murphys had not fully exhausted all of their administrative remedies because "access to immediate interim relief is essential for the vindication of this particular IDEA right [the "stay put" guarantee in § 1415(j)]."[75] With respect to the substantive issues, Judge Sotomayor relied on an intervening Second Circuit decision with a nearly identical fact pattern[76] and held that "Arlington is financially responsible for Joseph's tuition until such time as ... [his] placement is changed in accordance with the terms of the IDEA."[77] Finally, Judge Sotomayor found that the Murphys' *pro se* appearance at the district court was not reversible error, even though the Second Circuit does not permit non-attorney parents to represent their children.[78]

Finally, in *Mr. L. ex. rel. M. v. Sloan and Norwalk Board of Education,*[79] Judge Sotomayor addressed whether a party who prevailed in a purely private settlement agreement was entitled to attorneys' fees. IDEA allows a district court, in its discretion, to award attorneys' fees "to a prevailing party who is the parent of a child with a disability."[80] In this case, following a series of special education due process hearings, Mr. L., on behalf of his child M., and the Norwalk Board of Education reached a private settlement agreement concerning M.'s placement, and the hearing officer dismissed the case without approving the settlement or incorporating it into the order of dismissal. Mr. L., who had been the defendant in the due process hearings, then filed suit with the district court, arguing that he was a "prevailing party" and therefore entitled to recover attorneys' fees under IDEA. The district court held that Mr. L. was not a "prevailing party" and granted summary judgment to the school board. In her decision, Judge Sotomayor held that the decision in *Buckhannon Board and Care Home, Inc., v. West Virginia Department of Human Resources,*[81] which found that a "prevailing party" is one who achieves a judicially sanctioned change in the legal relationship of the parties,[82] applied "regardless of whether the party seeking fees is a plaintiff or a defendant" and therefore applied to this case.[83] She further held that the parties' settlement did not satisfy the *Buckhannon* requirement because it "was purely private and therefore does not constitute an administratively sanctioned change in the legal relationship of the parties that is judicially enforceable."[84] As a result Judge Sotomayor upheld the lower court's decision.

In addition to these written opinions, Judge Sotomayor joined in a unanimous ruling by the Second Circuit in *Board of Education of the Hyde Park Central School District v. Frank G.*[85] that held the family of a child with a disability could be reimbursed for private school tuition even if the child had never received services from the school district. This holding was later reached by the Supreme Court in a different case, *Forest Grove School District v. T.A.*[86] On June 22, 2009, the court held that IDEA authorized reimbursement for private special education services when a public school fails to provide FAPE and the private school placement is appropriate, regardless of whether the child previously received special education services through the public school. Prior to this decision, the court, dividing 4-4, in *Board of Education of the City School District of the City of New York v. Tom F.*[87] upheld a Second Circuit ruling on private school reimbursement. The court of appeals had held that parents of a child with a disability are entitled to private school reimbursement even though the student had never received special education services from the school district. However, the Court's *per curiam* decision was not precedent for lower courts, and the issue about whether reimbursement for private school tuition may be made when the child has not received public special education services was not settled by the Supreme Court until the *Forest Grove* decision.

Author Contact Information

Nancy Lee Jones
Legislative Attorney
njones@crs.loc.gov, 7-6976

Carol J. Toland
Legislative Attorney
ctoland@crs.loc.gov, 7-4659

End Notes

[1] 42 U.S.C. §12101 *et seq.*
[2] 29 U.S.C. §794.
[3] 42 U.S.C. §10801 et seq.
[4] 20 U.S.C. §1400 *et seq.*
[5] 2001 U.S. District LEXIS 11926 (S.D.N.Y. Aug. 15, 2001). See e.g., Jim Dwyer, "On the Bench with Fairness and Empathy," NEW YORK TIMES A-21 (May 27, 2009).
[6] See discussion *infra* pp. 3-5.
[7] See *Connecticut Office of Protection and Advocacy for Persons with Disabilities v. Hartford Board of Education,* 464 F.3d 229 (2d Cir. 2006).
[8] 1998 U.S. Dist. LEXIS 407 (S.D.N.Y. Jan. 21, 1998).
[9] See also *Lloret v. Lockwood Greene Engineers, Inc.,* 1998 U.S. Dist LEXIS 3999 (S.D.N.Y. 1998); *Brown v. arkchester South Condominiums*, 287 F.3d 58 (2d Cir. 2002); *Equal Employment Opportunity Commission v. J.B. Hunt Transport, Inc.*, 321 F.3d 69 (2d Cir. 2003).
[10] See, e.g., *Protection & Advocacy for Persons with Disabilities v. Mental Health & Addiction Services*, 448 F.3d 119 (2d Cir. 2006).
[11] See, e.g., *Bartlett v. New York State Board of Bar Examiners,* 1998 U.S. Dist. LEXIS 407 (S.D.N.Y. Jan. 21, 1998); *Norville v. Staten Island University,* 196 F.3d 89 (2d Cir. 1999); *Taylor v. Vermont Department of Education et al.*, 313 F.3d 768 (2d Cir. 2002).
[12] *Parker v. Columbia Pictures Industries*, 204 F.3d 326 (2d Cir. 2000); *Protection & Advocacy for Persons Disabilities v. Mental Health & Addiction Services,* 448 F.3d 119 (2d Cir. 2006).
[13] For a more detailed discussion of the ADA see CRS Report 98-921, *The Americans with Disabilities Act (ADA): Statutory Language and Recent Issues*, by Nancy Lee Jones.
[14] 42 U.S.C. §12101(b)(1).
[15] *Sutton v. United Air Lines, Inc.*, 527 U.S. 471 (1999); *Murphy v. United Parcel Service, Inc.*, 527 U.S. 516 (1999); *Albertsons, Inc. v. Kirkingburg*, 527 U.S. 555 (1999); *Toyota Motor Manufacturing v. Williams*, 534 U.S. 184 (2002).

[16] For a more detailed discussion of the ADA Amendments Act see CRS Report RL34691, *The ADA Amendments Act: P.L. 110-325*, by Nancy Lee Jones.
[17] 42 U.S.C. §12102(3).
[18] 42 U.S.C. 12102(4).
[19] 970 F. Supp. 1094 (S.D.N.Y. 1997) (opinion by Judge Sotomayor); reconsideration denied, 2 F.Supp.2d 388 (S.D.N.Y. 1997) (opinion by Judge Sotomayor); aff'd in part, vacated in part, 156 F.3d 321 (2d Cir. 1998); vacated remanded by 527 U.S. 1031 (1999); aff'd in part, vacated in part, remanded in part, 226 F.3d 69 (2d Cir. 2000); on remand, 2001 U.S. District LEXIS 11926 (S.D.N.Y. Aug. 15, 2001) (opinion by Judge Sotomayor, sitting by designation).
[20] *Id.*
[21] 970 F. Supp. 1094 (S.D.N.Y. 1997).
[22] 156 F.3d 321 (2d Cir. 1998).
[23] 527 U.S. 1031 (1999).
[24] 527 U.S. 471 (1999).
[25] 527 U.S. 516 (1999).
[26] 527 U.S. 555 (1999).
[27] 226 F.3d 69 (2d Cir. 2000).
[28] *Bartlett v. New York State Board of Law Examiners*, 2001 U.S. Dist. LEXIS 11926 (S.D.N.Y. August 15, 2001).
[29] A colloquy was held during the House debates on the ADA Amendments Act between Representatives Pete Stark and George Miller on the subject of the meaning of "substantially limits" in the context of learning, reading, writing, thinking, or speaking. The colloquy found that an individual who has performed well academically may still be considered an individual with a disability. 153 Cong. Rec. H. 8291 (September 17, 2008).
[30] 527 U.S. 555 (1999).
[31] P.L. 110-325 specifically states that the current Equal Employment Opportunity Commission (EEOC) regulations defining the term "substantially limits" as "significantly restricted" are "inconsistent with congressional intent, by expressing too high a standard." 42 U.S.C. §12101 note.
[32] See, e.g., "A multitude of people who manage their disabilities effectively through medication prosthetics, hearing aids, or other 'mitigating measures' are viewed as 'too functional'—or not 'disabled enough'—to be protected under the ADA.... It seems to me that the last message we would want to send to Americans with disabilities ... is the less you manage your disability, the less you try, the more likely you are to be protected under civil rights laws." Statement of Cheryl Sensenbrenner, Chair of the American Association of People with Disabilities, *ADA Restoration Act Hearing of 2007, Hearing on H.R. 3195 Before the Subcomm. on the Constitution, Civil Rights, and Civil Liberties of the H. Comm. on the Judiciary*, 110th Cong., at 25-26; quoted in H.REPT. 110-730, pt 2, at 10 (2008).
[33] 321 F.3d 69 (2d Cir. 2003).
[34] *Id.* at 80.
[35] 42 U.S.C. §12112(a).
[36] 42 U.S.C. §12111(5).
[37] 50 F. Supp. 2d 262 (S.D.N.Y. 1999).
[38] *Id.* at 290.
[39] *Id.* at 289.
[40] 204 F.3d 326 (2d Cir. 2000).
[41] *Id.* at 338.
[42] 42 U.S.C. §2000e-2(m).
[43] 196 F.3d 89 (2d Cir. 1999).
[44] *Id.* at 99.
[45] 1998 U.S. Dist. LEXIS 3999 (SDNY 1998).
[46] 287 F.3d 58 (2d Cir. 2002).
[47] 42 U.S.C. §§12131-12133.

[48] 339 F.3d 129 (2d Cir. 2003).
[49] 163 F.3d 729 (2d Cir. 1998).
[50] 29 U.S.C. §794.
[51] 1998 U.S.Dist. LEXIS 407 (S.D.N.Y. Jan. 21, 1998).
[52] 42 U.S.C. §10801(b).
[53] *Id.*
[54] 42 U.S.C. §10803.
[55] 42 U.S.C. §10805.
[56] 448 F.3d 119 (2d Cir. 2006).
[57] 464 F.3d 229 (2d Cir. 2006).
[58] 42 U.S.C. §15001 et seq.
[59] 29 U.S.C. §794(e).
[60] 20 U.S.C. §1400 et seq. For a detailed discussion of IDEA as amended by the 2004 reauthorization, see CRS Report RL32716, *Individuals with Disabilities Education Act (IDEA): Analysis of Changes Made by P.L. 108-446*, by Richard N. Apling and Nancy Lee Jones.
[61] For a more detailed discussion of the congressional intent behind the enactment of P.L. 94-142, see CRS Report 95- 669, *The Individuals with Disabilities Education Act: Congressional Intent*, by Nancy Lee Jones.
[62] Erik W. Robelen, "School Ruling by Sotomayor Eyed," EDUCATION WEEK (June 5, 2009), http://www.edweek.org/ew/articles/2009/06/10/33sotomayor2.h28.html?tkn=PXZFVopNh%2Bl lvMFiMtnJ1S6WDo5b9VocboEX&print=1, quoting Perry A. Zirkel, Professor of Education and Law at Lehigh University.
[63] 313 F.3d 768 (2d Cir. 2002).
[64] *Id.*
[65] 20 U.S.C. §1401(19)(A) (emphasis added).
[66] 34 C.F.R. §300.20.
[67] Taylor filed suit under IDEA and the Family Educational Rights and Privacy Act (FERPA). A discussion of the FERPA aspects of this case is beyond the scope of this report.
[68] 313 F.3d at 780.
[69] *Id.* at 782.
[70] *Id.* at 786.
[71] 297 F.3d 195 (2d Cir. 2002). Subsequent costs and fees proceedings in this case eventually reached the Supreme Court (*see* Arlington Central School District Board of Education v. Murphy, 548 U.S. 291), but the Supreme Court's decision did not involve issues decided by Judge Sotomayor's opinion.
[72] 20 U.S.C. §1415(j).
[73] *Id.* In enacting P.L. 94-142, the original version of IDEA, Congress provided grants to the states to help pay for education for children with disabilities, and also delineated specific requirements the states must follow to receive these federal funds. This public law contained a requirement that if there is a dispute between the school and the parents of a child with a disability, the child "stays put" in his or her current educational placement until the dispute is resolved using the due process procedures set forth in the statute. The concept of "stay put" was placed in the statute to help eliminate the then common discriminatory practice of expelling children with disabilities from school. A revised "stay put" provision remains as law in the current version of IDEA.
[74] 297 F.3d at 197.
[75] *Id.* at 200.
[76] Board of Education v. Schutz, 290 F.3d 476 (2d Cir. 2002).
[77] 297 F.3d at 201.
[78] *Id.* at 201.
[79] 449 F.3d 405 (2d Cir. 2006).
[80] 20 U.S.C. §1415(i)(3)(B)(i)(I).
[81] 532 U.S. 598 (2001).

[82] For more information about the *Buckhannon* decision, see CRS Report 98-921, *The Americans with Disabilities Act (ADA): Statutory Language and Recent Issues*, by Nancy Lee Jones.

[83] 449 F.3d at 407.

[84] *Id.* at 408.

[85] 459 F.3d 356 (2d Cir. 2006), *cert. den.,* 128 S. Ct. 436, 169 L. Ed. 2d 325, 2007 U.S. LEXIS 11520, 76 U.S.L.W. 3199 (U.S. 2007).

[86] 557 U.S. __ (2009), *aff'd* 523 F.3d 1078 (9th Cir. 2008).

[87] 552 U.S. 1 (2007), 128 S.Ct. 1, 199 L.Ed.2d 1 (2007).

In: Judge Sonia Sotomayor: Selected Options ISBN: 978-1-60876-759-5
Editors: Patrick K. Reed

Chapter 2

JUDGE SONIA SOTOMAYOR: ANALYSIS OF SELECTED OPINIONS

Anna C. Henning and Kenneth R. Thomas

SUMMARY

In May 2009, Supreme Court Justice David Souter announced his intention to retire from the Supreme Court. Several weeks later, President Obama nominated Judge Sonia Sotomayor, who currently serves on the U.S. Court of Appeals for the Second Circuit, to fill his seat. To fulfill its constitutional "advice and consent" function, the Senate will consider Judge Sotomayor's extensive record – compiled from years as a lawyer, prosecutor, district court judge, and appellate court judge – to better understand her legal approaches and judicial philosophy.

This report provides an analysis of selected opinions authored by Judge Sotomayor during her tenure as a judge on the Second Circuit. Discussions of the selected opinions are grouped according to various topics of legal significance.

As a group, the opinions belie easy categorization along any ideological spectrum. However, it is possible to draw some conclusions regarding Judge Sotomayor's judicial approach, both within some specific issue areas and in general.

Perhaps the most consistent characteristic of Judge Sotomayor 's approach as an appellate judge has been an adherence to the doctrine of *stare decisis*, i.e., the upholding of past judicial precedents. Other characteristics appear to include what many would describe as a careful application of particular facts at issue in a case and a dislike for situations in which the court might be seen as oversteping its judicial role.

It is difficult to determine the extent to which Judge Sotomayor 's style as a judge on the Second Circuit would predict her style should she become a Supreme Court justice. However, as has been the case historically with other nominees, some of her approaches may be enduring characteristics.

INTRODUCTION

On May 26, 2009, President Obama nominated Judge Sonia Sotomayor of the U.S. Court of Appeals for the Second Circuit to fill the Supreme Court seat that will be vacated by retiring Justice David Souter. Judge Sotomayor has served on the Second Circuit since 1998. Before her appointment to the Second Circuit, she served as a federal district court judge for the U.S. District Court for the Southern District of New York. Prior to her role on the federal bench, she worked as a prosecutor and spent several years as an attorney in private practice.

This report analyzes selected cases authored by Judge Sotomayor during her tenure on the Second Circuit, including majority, concurring, and dissenting opinions in areas of legal significance. In some instances, it also discusses an opinion authored by Judge Sotomayor while she was a district court judge or a *per curiam* ("by the court") opinion for which Judge Sotomayor served on the panel of judges that ruled in the case.

Overall, Judge Sotomayor's opinions defy easy categorization along ideological lines. In particular areas, a general substantive approach may be discerned. For example, her appellate court opinions in cases involving suits by individuals with disabilities could be seen as appearing to favor plaintiffs' claims, and in various areas of international concern, she could be said to have shown a tendency to make the Second Circuit available to plaintiffs unless circuit precedent and the political branches have indicated otherwise.

General characteristics of her approach to the judicial role are more easily identified. Perhaps the most consistent characteristic of Judge Sotomayor 's approach as an appellate judge could be described as an adherence to the doctrine of *stare decisis*, i.e., the upholding of past judicial precedents. This characteristic would be in line with the judicial philosophy of Justice Souter, who often displayed special respect for upholding past precedent.[1] Another characteristic of Judge Sotomayor 's opinions could be described as a meticulous evaluation of the particular facts at issue in a case, which may inform whether past judicial precedents from the circuit are applicable. Her approach to statutory interpretation seems similarly nuanced. She tends to adhere to the plain meaning of the text but, in the face of ambiguous language, appears willing to consider the intent and purpose of a statute. Judge Sotomayor 's opinions also display her apparent dislike for situations in which the court oversteps the role called for by the procedural posture of a case. For example, in a dissenting opinion in a Fourth Amendment case, issued in May 2009, she wrote that the court had overstepped its role by delving into the facts in a case involving review of a denial of a motion for summary judgment.[2]

While many of her judicial approaches may be enduring, some shifts in her legal conclusions may naturally arise because of the difference in the roles of a circuit court judge versus a Supreme Court justice. Whereas circuit court decisions are often bound by relevant Supreme Court precedents, the Supreme Court more often considers issues of "first impression" – i.e., issues for which no relevant precedent governs the outcome. In addition, Supreme Court justices have greater control over their docket than do circuit court judges, and they review cases originating state and federal courts throughout the nation. In contrast, as a judge on the Second Circuit, Judge in Sotomayor has typically reviewed cases that originated in federal courts in Vermont, New York, and Connecticut.

The jurisdictional area and the nature of the Second Circuit affects the range of subjects in which Judge Sotomayor has had an opportunity to author opinions as an appellate judge. For example, because none of the states in the Second Circuit's area authorizes the death penalty, she has not has been called upon to review a case involving a death sentence. Nonetheless, during her more than a decade on the Second Circuit, she has written opinions in many issue areas that may be of interest to the Senate during its deliberations. The following discussion analyzes pertinent opinions authored by Judge Sotomayor in several of these areas.

FIRST AMENDMENT: FREE SPEECH[3]

The First Amendment of the Constitution provides that "Congress shall make no law ... abridging the freedom of speech, or of the press.... "[4] Judge Sotomayor 's decisions interpreting this clause do not appear to be considered particularly controversial. To the extent that a pattern can be discerned, some might point to a meticulous recitation of the facts and her application of precedent from the

Supreme Court or the Second Circuit to those facts.[5] Consequently, it does not appear possible to discern a particular ideology from her opinions or to determine whether she would favor a more or less expansive application of the Free Speech Clause of the First Amendment.

For example, in *Center for Reproductive Law and Policy v. Bush*,[6] Judge Sotomayor, writing for the Second Circuit, dismissed a First Amendment challenge to the "Mexico City Policy," which restricted foreign non-governmental family planning organizations in receipt of U.S. funds from providing or promoting abortions. The Center for Reproductive Law and Policy ("CLRP") argued that the policy restricted its First Amendment right to communicate with foreign nongovernmental family planning organizations that fell under these prohibitions. Judge Sotomayor applied Second Circuit precedent that had dismissed a nearly identical challenge to the policy and found that the Mexico City policy did not prevent the CLRP from exercising its first amendment rights. On the other hand, in *U.S. v. Quattrone*,[7] in another opinion authored by Judge Sotomayor, the Second Circuit overturned a gag rule placed upon the press by the district court. Sotomayor noted that the gag order was a prior restraint and that such speech suppression is among the least tolerated forms of suppression under the First Amendment. Applying Supreme Court precedent articulated in *Nebraska Press Association v. Stuart*,[8] Sotomayor held that the district court had not sufficiently justified the gag order and thus overturned it.

Another case analyzing the constitutionality of a prior restraint was *Doe v. Mukasey*.[9] Judge Sotomayor was part of a unanimous three-judge panel that declared portions of the USA PATRIOT Act unconstitutional. The case considered provisions of the act that prohibited recipients of national security letters (NSLs) from disclosing the fact that they had received the letters, an issue on which the Supreme Court has yet to speak directly. The panel, therefore, applied Supreme Court precedent related to prior restraints articulated in *Freedman v. Maryland*.[10] The panel, however, appeared to do so with attention to Supreme Court decisions that indicate courts owe a higher degree of deference to the Executive Branch in matters of national security.[11]

In *Freedman*, the Supreme Court held that, in general, where an expression is conditioned on government permission, three procedural protections are needed to guard against impermissible censorship: (1) restraint prior to judicial review must be only for "a specified brief period"; (2) any further restraint prior to a final judicial determination must be limited to "the shortest fixed period compatible with sound judicial resolution"; and (3) the burden of going to court to suppress speech and the burden of proof in court must be placed on the government.[12] The Second Circuit was able to construe most of the provisions at issue to avoid constitutional difficulties related to the first two requirements. However, the panel found that one of the provisions of the act contradicted *Freedman*'s third requirement regarding the burden of bringing an action.

Another provision of the act treated certification on the part of government officials that the disclosure might endanger national security or interfere with diplomatic relations as conclusive evidence to sustain the government's burden of proof. The panel held that a certification was not enough to meet the burden of proof standard set out in *Freedman*. The panel, therefore, partially invalidated the provisions at issue, but did not find the provisions to be unconstitutional in their entirety. Instead, the panel remanded the case to allow the government the opportunity to comply with the proper constitutional standards.

Speech of Government Employees

In *Pappas v. Giuliani*,[13] Judge Sotomayor demonstrated a willingness to express a difference of opinion on the application of precedent to a set of facts, albeit without appearing to step outside the bounds of established case law. A majority of a panel of judges on the Second Circuit upheld the decision of the New York City Police Department (NYPD) to fire an officer for expressing racist sentiments against a First Amendment challenge. The officer's speech was made in anonymous writings that he sent in reply to solicitations for charitable donations, and the speech was not made in relationship to his employment. Under Supreme Court precedent, public against employees because they expressed their opinions on matters of public concern.[14] However, employees' freedom to speak on matters of public concern is balanced against the state's interest in the performance of its functions. Applying this standard, the court held that the interests of the police department outweighed Pappas' free speech rights in this case. The court found that public knowledge of a New York City police officer expressing racist attitudes could substantially undermine the mission of the police department, and the interest in maintaining an effective police department outweighed Officer Pappas' speech rights and any effort Pappas may have undertaken to remain anonymous.

Judge Sotomayor dissented.[15] She applied the same precedent as the majority, but reached a different conclusion. In her opinion, the nature of Pappas' job and the fact that he had spoken anonymously should have tipped the balance in Pappas' favor despite the fact that she found his speech to be "patently offensive, hateful, and insulting."[16] Judge Sotomayor argued that not only must a court consider a government entity's mission in relation to an employee's speech, a court must also consider the nature of that employee's position within the government entity. She then examined the nature of Pappas' job and found that, though he was an officer, he was not a cop on the beat in contact with the public or a high-ranking policy official. Because his job was not to set policy or to be in contact with the public, she argued that his private opinions about race would not undermine the NYPD's ability to function, even if his attitude became public. Judge Sotomayor also found it significant that the speech in question occurred away from work, on the employee's own time, and anonymously. She was swayed by the fact that the employee's speech was only brought to light as a result of the employer's investigation and the employer's decision to publicize its results. She noted that the verdict in this case could allow government employers to launch investigations into employees' speech and fire them for views that had been anonymously expressed: a result that she found to be a perversion of the reasonable belief standard – i.e., the requirement that the government must have "reasonably believed that the speech would potentially ... disrupt the government's acitivities."[17] Taken together, Judge Sotomayor determined from these findings that Pappas had established a claim for retaliation.

In *Singh v. City of New York*, [18] another retaliation suit involving the speech of a government employee, Judge Sotomayor, writing for a unanimous panel, ruled against the employee. Singh worked as a fire alarm inspector and was required to carry certain documents with him to and from home each day. He voiced his opinion in a number of ways that he should be compensated for his travel time to and from work each day. Sotomayor found that Singh's speech did not involve a matter of public concern, because it could not "be fairly characterized as relating to any matter of political, social, or other concern to the community."[19] According to Judge Sotomayor, Singh's speech related only to internal employment policies and could not establish the first element of a First Amendment retaliation claim – i.e., that his speech addressed a matter of public concern.

Prisoner Speech Rights

Judge Sotomayor showed significant deference to prison officials making security decisions in *Duamutef v. Hollins*.[20] In that case, prison officials had placed an inmate on "mail watch" after he received a book entitled, "Blood in the Streets: Investment Profits in a World Gone Mad." In an opinion authored by Judge Sotomayor, the Second Circuit held that, though the contents of the book were harmless, due to the prisoner's history of subversive behavior and the provocative nature of the title, prison officials could restrict the prisoner's mail. This case appears to grant prison officials wide discretion to place restrictions upon prisoners' First Amendment rights, provided the officials have some reason to believe such restrictions would benefit prison security.

Student Speech

While Judge Sotomayor did not author any opinions dealing with the free speech rights of students, she did sit on panels that heard two notable cases. Both cases applied Supreme Court school speech precedents which held that student speech which is not school sponsored, offensive or inappropriate can only be restricted if it would substantially disrupt the school function.[21] In *Guiles v. Marineau*,[22] Judge Sotomayor joined a panel ruling in favor of the student, finding that his anti-President Bush T-shirt had not disrupted the functioning of his school. On the other hand, in *Doninger v. Niehoff*, [23] the panel, including Judge Sotomayor, ruled in favor of a school which had disciplined a student for speech she had engaged in off-campus, finding that the speech did cause substantial disruption to school function. These cases would seem to indicate that Judge Sotomayor has not demonstrated a clear preference between the free speech rights of students versus a school's discretion to discipline.

FIRST AMENDMENT: RELIGION[24]

While on the Second Circuit, Sotomayor has authored few opinions related to religious freedom, and her opinions in the area do not appear controversial. However, as issues related to the First Amendment's religion clause often appear on the Supreme Court docket,[25] Judge Sotomayor's record in such cases will likely be of interest.

Religious Freedom Restoration Act

In a case involving the scope of application of the Religious Freedom Restoration Act (RFRA), Judge Sotomayor authored a dissent, arguing that the court had misapplied RFRA and violated the principle of judicial restraint. In *Hankins v. Lyght*, [26] a minister who was forced by his church to retire due to age limits filed a lawsuit under the Age Discrimination in Employment Act (ADEA). The Second Circuit held that RFRA, a statute that generally prohibits the government from placing substantial burdens on religious exercise, amended the ADEA and remanded the case to the district court for a hearing on the merits of the case.[27] Judge Sotomayor dissented, arguing that the court's opinion violated principles of judicial restraint because RFRA was not raised as an issue in the case.[28] She also argued that RFRA should not be applied in a dispute between private parties and indicated her agreement with other circuits' adoption of a ministerial exception to anti-discrimination laws, which allows religious organizations to select clergy without regard to anti-discrimination requirements.[29]

The issue in *Lyght*—the freedom of religious organizations to have independence in hiring decisions, even if those decisions would otherwise violate federal anti-discrimination laws—has been a recurring one. Although it has been considered by some lower courts, it has not yet reached the Supreme Court. The Department of Justice under the Bush administration applied RFRA to protect such actions by religious organizations, asserting that anti-discrimination requirements imposed a substantial burden on religious organizations' exercise of religion.[30] The debate over religious organizations' so-called hiring rights continues to be controversial, especially in cases where an organization has received public funding for social service programs.

Prisoner Free Exercise Rights

Another recurring First Amendment issue involves instances in which the government is alleged to have denied prisoners' religious free exercise rights. Courts are generally deferential to the government regarding the degree of accommodation owed to inmates, as exceptions to prison rules and regulations are difficult to enforce while maintaining order within the prison system.[31]

While on the Second Circuit, however, Judge Sotomayor wrote opinions in two prisoner free exercise cases – *Ford v. McGinnis* and *Salahuddin v. Mead*[32] – that held in favor of the prisoners.

While the facts of those cases were not particularly controversial, Sotomayor's opinions in these cases may provide insight into her judicial perspective on religious free exercise generally. Free exercise cases generally require the claimant to have a sincere religious belief and require that the action challenged impose a substantial burden on that belief. In one of the prisoner free exercise opinions, Judge Sotomayor strongly emphasized the importance of using a subjective definition of religion in evaluating such beliefs. Suggesting that an objective belief test "would require courts to resolve questions that are beyond their competence," Sotomayor wrote that the subjective definition "examines an individual's inward attitudes towards a particular belief system" and that "the freedom to exercise religious beliefs cannot be made contingent on the objective truth of such beliefs."[33]

Judge Sotomayor also noted the current circuit split over whether or not the substantial burden test should apply in prisoner free exercise cases, but did not indicate a preference for either position. She did discuss standards by which courts measure whether a substantial burden exists, which is a central issue in a non-prisoner case that has been submitted to the Court for possible review.[34] Judge Sotomayor again emphasized the idea that "courts are particularly ill-suited" to "distinguish important from unimportant religious beliefs."[35] She rejected a narrow definition of substantial burden which has been favored by some circuits that would define substantial burden as a burden on a practice mandated by the religion.[36] Instead, Sotomayor framed the substantial burden analysis as whether the relevant religious belief is considered central or important to the individual's practice of his or her religion.[37]

SECOND AMENDMENT: INCORPORATION[38]

On June 26, 2008, the Supreme Court issued its decision in *District of Columbia v. Heller,*[39] holding by a 5-4 vote that the Second Amendment protects an individual right to possess a firearm, unconnected to service in a militia, and protects the right to use that firearm for traditional lawful purposes such as self-defense within the home. In *Heller*, the Court affirmed a lower court's holding that declared three provisions of the District of Columbia's Firearms Control Regulation Act unconstitutional.[40] Although the Court did an extensive analysis of the Second Amendment to interpret the meaning of the Second Amendment, the decision left unanswered many questions of significant constitutional magnitude, including the standard of scrutiny that should be applied to laws regulating the possession and use of firearms, and whether the Second Amendment applies to the states. It is the latter issue which has been most commented upon by lower courts in post-*Heller* cases.

Over 100 years ago, the Court held in *United States v. Cruikshank*[41] (and reaffirmed in *Presser v. Illinois)*[42] that the Second Amendment does not act as a constraint upon state law. Both of these decisions, however, were decided prior to the advent of modern incorporation principles. The Court in *Heller* briefly commented upon the issue of incorporation stating, "[w]ith respect to *Cruikshank's* continuing validity on incorporation, a question not presented by this case, we note that *Cruikshank* also said that the First Amendment did not apply against the States and did not engage in the sort of Fourteenth Amendment inquiry required by our later cases."[43] It further noted that subsequent Supreme Court cases had reaffirmed the holding that the Second Amendment applies only to the federal government.[44] While these statements could be viewed as indicating that the Court would continue with this precedent, it could also be interpreted as indicating that the Court would support the application of modern incorporation doctrine principles to the Second Amendment.

Since the *Heller* decision, three federal appellate circuits have addressed whether the Second Amendment applies to the states. The first decision to address this issue was a three-judge *per curiam* opinion by the Second Circuit in *Maloney v. Rice,*[45] in which Judge Sotomayor was one of the judges. In *Maloney*, the plaintiff sought a declaration that a New York penal law that punishes the possession of nunchukas[46] was unconstitutional. On appeal, the plaintiff argued that the state statutory ban violates the Second Amendment because it infringes on his right to keep and bear arms. Here, the court, citing *Presser v. Illinois*, held that the state law did not violate the Second Amendment because "it is settled law ... that the Second Amendment applies only to limitations the federal government seeks to impose on this right."[47] The court noted that, although *Heller* might have questioned the continuing validity of this principle, Supreme Court precedent directs them to follow *Presser* because "[w]here, as here, a Supreme Court precedent 'has direct application in a case, yet appears to rest on reasons rejected in some other line of decisions, the Court of Appeals should follow the case which directly controls, leaving to the Supreme Court the prerogative of overruling its own decisions.'"[48]

After the Second Circuit decision, the U.S. Court of Appeals for the Ninth Circuit in *Nordyke v. King* held the opposite and concluded that the Due Process Clause of the Fourteenth Amendment incorporates the Second Amendment and applied it against the states and local governments.[49] The court stated that there are three doctrinal ways the Second Amendment could apply to the states: (1) direct application; (2) incorporation by the Privileges and Immunities Clause of the Fourteenth Amendment, or (3) incorporation by the Due Process Clause of the Fourteenth Amendment. The court held that it was precluded from finding incorporation through the first two options and embarked on an analysis under the Due Process Clause by determining whether the right under the Second Amendment is "deeply rooted in this Nation's history and tradition."[50] After engaging in an historical analysis of the right during the Founding era, the post-Revolutionary years, and the post-Civil War era, the court concluded that the Second Amendment was incorporated because "the crucial role [of this] deeply rooted right ... compels us to recognize that it is indeed fundamental [and] necessary to the Anglo-American conception of the ordered liberty that we have inherited."[51]

On June 2, 2009, the United States Court of Appeals for the Seventh Circuit issued its decision in *National Rifle Ass'n of America v. City of Chicago and Village of Oak Park*.[52] Here, the Seventh Circuit followed the Second Circuit and also held that the Second Amendment does not apply to the states. Like the Second Circuit, the Seventh Circuit stated that the Supreme Court's decisions in *Cruikshank*, *Presser*, and *Miller* still control as they have direct application in the case. The court noted that, although *Heller* questioned *Cruikshank*, this "[did] not license inferior courts to go their own ways.... If a court of appeals may strike off on its own, this not only undermines the uniformity of national law but also may compel the Justices to grant certiorari before they think the question ripe for decision."[53]

ARTICLE I: COMMERCE CLAUSE[54]

While on the Second Circuit, Judge Sotomayor has had an opportunity to address federalism issues, although it does not appear that these cases are considered of particular significance. For instance, in *United States v. Giordano*,[55] the court held that the then-mayor of Waterbury, Connecticut had been constitutionally convicted of making telephone calls to solicit sex with minors, despite the fact that some of these calls had occurred entirely within Connecticut. Writing for the court, Judge Sotomayor held that 18 U.S.C. §2425, which prohibits the use of "any facility or means of interstate or foreign commerce," to transmit contact information regarding a person under the age of 16 years with the intent of that person engaging in illegal sexual activity, could constitutionally be applied to intrastate phone calls, because the law at issue related to an instrumentality of commerce.

The *Giordana* case is within mainstream Commerce Clause analysis.[56] In *United States v. Lopez*,[57] the Supreme Court identified three different categories of regulation in which the commerce power could be exercised: (1) regulation of channels of commerce; (2) regulation of instrumentalities of commerce; and (3) regulation of economic activities that have an "effect" on commerce. Using this framework, the *Lopez* Court struck down the Gun-Free School Zones Act of 1990, which made it illegal for "any individual knowingly to possess a firearm at a place that the individual knows, or has reasonable cause to believe, is a school zone."[58]

The Court in *Lopez* reasoned that the law did not fall under the first two commerce categories, but it also found that it had no substantial "effect" (the third category) on commercial transactions, either by itself or in the aggregate. Further, the statute contained no requirement that interstate commerce be affected, such as that the gun had been previously transported in interstate commerce. Nor was the criminalization of possession of a gun near a school part of a larger regulatory scheme that did regulate commerce.

It should be noted that the analysis of *Lopez* dealt principally with the "effect" category of Commerce Clause analysis, not the "channels" or "instrumentalities" of commerce categories. At least two federal courts of appeals have suggested, however, that where the relationship between a "channels" or "instrumentalities" regulation and commercial activity is attenuated, that there may also need to be some additional Commerce Clause nexus.[59] This line of reasoning, however, has not generally been used in the context of a highly regulated interstate instrumentality such as the telephone network at issue in *Giordana.* Thus, Judge Sotomayor, relying on past precedent in the circuit, did not address this alternative line of analysis.

It may be noted, however, that Judge Sotomayor did not appear inclined to focus on the alternative line of reasoning, even when some might consider it relevant to another case decided by the Second Circuit. In *United States v. Harris,* the Court considered 18 U.S.C. § 252A(a)(5)(B), which prohibits:

> Knowingly possess[ing] any book, magazine, periodical, film, videotape, computer disk, or any other material that contains an image of child pornography that has been mailed, or shipped or transported in interstate or foreign commerce by any means, including by computer, or that was produced using materials that have been mailed, or shipped or transported.

Other circuits had evaluated this statute under the "effect" category, and had found that regulation of mere possession of pornography where no commercial activity was involved was insufficient to meet the requirements set forth by the Supreme Court.[60] These cases seemed to conclude that the fact that the materials to make the pornography had moved in "channels" of commerce (the second category) did not preclude the application of the more rigorous requirements established for the "effects" prong of Commerce Clause jurisprudence.

It should be noted that the Supreme Court has not adopted these changes to its Commerce Clause doctrine as it relates to "channels" and "instrumentalities" of commerce, and Supreme Court *dicta* does not appear to support such a change.[61] Further, the Court's decision in the case of *Gonzales v. Raich* seems to indicate that, to the extent that a prohibition against the possession of illegal contraband is important to a larger regulatory scheme restricting the sale or manufacture of such contraband, it is likely to fall within the Necessary and Proper Clause.[62]

Judge Sotomayor 's decision in *Harris*, however, did not directly evaluate the alternative line of Court of Appeals cases striking down 18 U.S.C. § 2252A(a)(5)(B).[63] Instead, her opinion relied on prior Second Circuit precedent considering a prohibition on child pornography. In *United States v. Holston,*[64] the Second Circuit upheld a prohibition on production (not possession) of pornographic depictions based on *Lopez* and its progeny. In evaluating the relevance of *Holston*, Judge Sotomayor noted that, for purposes of Commerce Clause analysis, she saw no distinction between the possession of pornography and its production. Consequently, she found that no further analysis was necessary and upheld the prohibition. [65]

ARTICLE II: EXECUTIVE POWER[66]

In recent years, the Supreme Court has considered several cases involving national security. These cases have typically concerned the scope of executive authority in the conflict with Al Qaeda and the Taliban, as well as the rights owed to persons detained by the United States in the course of the conflict. Court rulings in this area have often been made by a five-justice majority.[67] As a result, there has been significant interest in Judge Sotomayor 's views regarding national security. If she is confirmed, it is possible that she would cast a deciding vote in national security cases that come before the Supreme Court in the coming years.

An examination of Judge Sotomayor 's opinions provides little guidance as to her judicial philosophy regarding executive authority in the realm of national security. During her tenure with the Second Circuit, Judge Sotomayor has heard only a handful of cases concerning national security matters. As will be discussed later,[68] Judge Sotomayor wrote an opinion in 2006 for a unanimous three-judge panel in *Cassidy v. Chertoff,* [69] holding that minimally intrusive, suspicionless searches of passengers' carry-on baggage and automobile trunks before boarding a commuter ferry were justified on account of the government's interest in deterring terrorist attacks on large vessels involved in mass transportation. Also, as discussed previously,[70] Judge Sotomayor joined a unanimous three-judge opinion in 2008 striking down on First Amendment grounds two provisions of the USA PATRIOT Act relating to the disclosure of the receipt of National Security Letters.[71] These cases, however, provide little indication as to how Judge Sotomayor might rule on broader national security issues relating to executive power or the detention of suspected terrorists.

A case currently before an *en banc* panel of the Second Circuit may provide further guidance as to Judge Sotomayor's views toward executive power on matters related to national security. The case of *Arar v. Ashcroft* concerns a civil suit filed by a dual citizen of Canada and Syria who was apprehended by U.S. immigration authorities during a flight layover at New York's John F. Kennedy International Airport and thereafter removed to Syria. Arar brought suit against certain U.S. officials that he claims were responsible for transferring him to Syria, where he was allegedly tortured and interrogated, with the acquiescence of the United States, for suspected terrorist activities (Arar 's transfer has sometimes been characterized as an "extraordinary rendition"). In 2006, the U.S. District Court for the Eastern District of New York dismissed Arar's civil case on a number of grounds, including that certain claims raised against U.S. officials implicated national security and foreign policy considerations, and assessing the propriety of those considerations was most appropriately reserved to Congress and the executive branch.[72] A three-judge panel of the Court of Appeals for the Second Circuit upheld the lower court's dismissal in 2008,[73] but the circuit court subsequently agreed to rehear the case sitting *en banc*. Although the circuit court has heard oral arguments in the case,[74] it has yet to issue a final decision. Presuming that Judge Sotomayor participates in the court's final ruling, her decision may shed further light as to her views on judicial oversight regarding executive action in the field of national security.

CIVIL RIGHTS: GENERALLY[75]

Judge Sotomayor has authored a number of opinions in the area of civil rights. Although these cases all involve claims of discrimination, such claims are made under a wide array of federal, state, and local laws that vary significantly in the types of bias they prohibit and the classes of individuals they protect. As a result, it is difficult to detect a pattern in Judge Sotomayor 's civil rights rulings. Indeed, of the seven opinions she has authored in the area of civil rights, Judge

Sotomayor has ruled in favor of the party claiming discrimination in three of them and against the party claiming discrimination in four others.

Meanwhile, Judge Sotomayor 's stance in *Ricci v. DeStafano*,[76] a case involving allegations of reverse discrimination by a group of white firefighters, is somewhat more ambiguous. Although *Ricci* is perhaps the most well known of the civil rights cases in which she has participated, Judge Sotomayor did not issue a written opinion in the case. Rather, a three-judge panel of the Second Circuit that included Judge Sotomayor issued a one-paragraph unsigned opinion that summarily affirmed the district court's decision. Nevertheless, the case is significant because the Supreme Court has agreed to review the decision and is expected to issue its ruling before the end of its term in June.[77]

In *Ricci*, city officials in New Haven, Connecticut declined to certify a promotional test on which black and Hispanic firefighters had performed poorly relative to white firefighters. Several white and Hispanic firefighters sued, claiming that the city's actions violated, among other laws, Title VII of the Civil Rights Act of 1964, which prohibits discrimination in employment on the basis of race, color, national origin, sex, or religion,[78] and the Equal Protection Clause of the Fourteenth Amendment, which prohibits a state from denying equal protection to its citizens.[79] City officials defended their actions, arguing that Title VII prohibits employment policies or practices that have a disparate racial impact and that the city was in fact attempting to comply with Title VII and avoid a lawsuit when it refused to certify test results that had a disparate impact on minority firefighters.

The district court ultimately sided with the City of New Haven, holding that the "[d]efendants' motivation to avoid making promotions based on a test with a racially disparate impact ... does not ... as a matter of law, constitute discriminatory intent, and therefore such evidence is insufficient for plaintiffs to prevail on their Title VII claim."[80] Likewise, the district court rejected the plaintiffs' equal protection claim, ruling that the city's attempt to remedy the disparate impact of the test did not constitute an intent to discriminate against the non-minority firefighters and that the rejection of the test results did not amount to an unlawful racial classification because all applicants were treated the same with respect to the administration and invalidation of the tests.[81]

As noted above, a three-judge panel of the Second Circuit that included Judge Sotomayor issued a one-paragraph affirmation of the "well-reasoned opinion" of the district court, noting that because the city "in refusing to validate the exams, was simply trying to fulfill its obligations under Title VII when confronted with test results that had a disproportionate racial impact, its actions were protected."[82] Neither Judge Sotomayor nor the other judges provided additional insight into their legal reasoning in the decision. The case has drawn considerable attention, however, not only because of the controversial nature of the reverse discrimination allegations but also because some observers expect the Supreme Court to reverse the Second Circuit's decision.[83]

Although it is difficult to characterize Judge Sotomayor 's decision in *Ricci*, her written opinions in other civil rights cases provide more insight into her legal reasoning. Several of these cases have been decided at least in part in favor of the party claiming discrimination. For example, in *Raniola v. Bratton*,[84] the Second Circuit considered, among other claims, allegations of sex discrimination under Title VII made by a female police officer who had been terminated from her job. The district court had dismissed the officer's hostile work environment and retaliation claims as a matter of law, but Judge Sotomayor, writing for a unanimous three-judge panel, reversed the lower court. Applying the standard that governs when parties move for judgment as a matter of law—to review the evidence in the light most favorable to the nonmoving party—Judge Sotomayor examined evidence of verbal abuse, disparate treatment on the basis of sex, and workplace sabotage and concluded that "[t]he evidence which Raniola presented and the additional witness testimony that Raniola proffered provide a sufficient basis for a reasonable jury to conclude that Raniola was subjected to a hostile work environment because she was a woman and that Raniola was suspended, put on probation, and then terminated in retaliation for having complained of her treatment."[85] It is important to note that Judge Sotomayor's ruling did not constitute a decision on the merits of the claim. Rather, by remanding the case to the lower court for trial, Judge Sotomayor left the ultimate decision on the plaintiff's claims of sex discrimination and retaliation to a jury.

Similarly, in *Cruz v. Coach Stores*,[86] the Second Circuit reviewed a Hispanic female plaintiff's allegations of race and sex discrimination under various federal, state, and local laws. Although Judge Sotomayor, writing for a unanimous three-judge panel, upheld the district court's rejection of virtually all of the plaintiff's claims – including claims regarding failure to promote, retaliation, discriminatory termination, and disparate impact – the judge did reverse the district court's grant of summary judgment with respect to the plaintiff's hostile work environment claim. Judge Sotomayor found that, unlike the other claims, the plaintiff had "established a genuine factual dispute regarding her claim of hostile work environment harassment" on the basis of race and sex when her allegations were viewed in the most favorable light.[87] Specifically, the plaintiff had cited repeated evidence of racial slurs by her supervisor, as well as evidence of physical and verbal sexual harassment. Notably, the district court appeared to consider the evidence of sexual harassment to be too vague or isolated, but Judge Sotomayor concluded that "the physically threatening nature of [the supervisor's] behavior, which repeatedly ended with him backing Cruz into the wall ... brings this case over the line separating merely offensive or boorish conduct from actionable sexual harassment."[88] The judge also emphasized that "a jury could find that [the supervisor's] racial harassment exacerbated the effect of his sexually threatening behavior and vice versa."[89] As a result, although Judge Sotomayor rejected the majority of the plaintiff's claims of discrimination, she remanded the case for trial for an ultimate decision on the merits of the hostile work environment claim.

Unlike the two decisions above, which were unanimous, Judge Sotomayor's written opinion in the remaining case in which she sided at least in part with the party claiming discrimination was a dissenting opinion. In *Grant v. Wallingford Board of Education*,[90] the Second Circuit examined a case involving an elementary school student who alleged race discrimination under 42 U.S.C. §§ 1981 and 1983, two civil rights statutes that provide a remedy for various types of discrimination.[91] Specifically, the plaintiff claimed that school officials intentionally discriminated against him through deliberate indifference to racial hostility in the classroom and through a decision to transfer him from first grade to kindergarten mid-way through the year. All three judges on the panel agreed that there was insufficient evidence to support the student's claim of racial hostility, but Judge Sotomayor vigorously dissented from the majority's ruling that the plaintiff's claim of a discriminatory transfer lacked merit. According to the judge, the plaintiff, who was the only black child in his class and one of only a few black children in the entire school, had presented evidence that his transfer was "unprecedented and contrary to the school's established policies" and that he had suffered disparate treatment as compared to similarly situated white students who had received transitional assistance rather than transfers when experiencing academic difficulties.[92] As a result, Judge Sotomayor reasoned that the plaintiff's evidence of race discrimination was sufficient for a reasonable jury to reach a verdict in his favor and she therefore would have remanded the case for trial on the question of the classroom transfer.

In contrast to the cases described above, Judge Sotomayor has also authored several civil rights opinions in which she ruled or would have ruled against the party claiming discrimination. For example, in *Williams v. R.H. Donnelly Co.*,[93] the Second Circuit considered a black female employee's claim that her employer had violated Title VII's prohibition against race and sex discrimination by denying her various promotions, refusing to transfer her, and failing to create a management position for her. Writing for a unanimous three-judge panel, Judge Sotomayor affirmed the district court's grant of summary judgment to the employer. Specifically, the judge determined that the plaintiff had failed to establish that she was qualified for the promotions she sought, had failed to prove that her employer's refusal to create a position for her was motivated by discrimination, and had failed to demonstrate that the denial of a transfer to a lesser position constituted an adverse employment action, all prerequisites to establishing her claims.[94]

Likewise, in *Norville v. Staten Island University Hospital*,[95] Judge Sotomayor authored a unanimous opinion rejecting race and age discrimination claims brought under state and local laws by an older black female nurse. With regard to the race discrimination claim, Judge Sotomayor held that the plaintiff had failed to produce evidence sufficient to support a reasonable inference of race discrimination, in part because she had not demonstrated that similarly situated employees of a different race were treated differently. With regard to the age discrimination claim, the judge held that the plaintiff had successfully established a prima facie case of discrimination but had failed to prove that the hospital's explanation for its actions were a pretext for discrimination, as required by legal precedents.

In *Washington v. County of Rockland*,[96] the Second Circuit reviewed the claims of a group of black corrections officers who alleged, among other things, that prison officials were illegally motivated by race in violation of 42 U.S.C. §§ 1981 and 1983 when they pursued administrative disciplinary proceedings against the officers. The district court held that the plaintiffs failed to file their race discrimination claims in a timely manner, and Judge Sotomayor, writing for a unanimous three-judge panel, affirmed, ruling that the plaintiffs had not sued until after the statute of limitations had expired.

Finally, as discussed earlier,[97] in *Hankins v. Lyght*,[98] the Second Circuit considered a claim brought under the Age Discrimination in Employment Act (ADEA) by a minister who was forced to retire under his church's mandatory retirement policy. The district court dismissed the case, but a majority of the three-judge panel reversed, ruling that the Religious Freedom Restoration Act (RFRA), which generally bars the government from substantially burdening an individual's free exercise of religion, effectively amended the ADEA. The majority therefore remanded the case to the district court for reconsideration under the RFRA standards.

However, Judge Sotomayor dissented, arguing that RFRA did not apply to the dispute. She expressly criticized the majority for "violat[ing] a cardinal principle of judicial restraint" by examining RFRA's constitutionality,[99] and she disagreed with several of the majority's legal conclusions regarding the applicability of the statute.[100] In particular, Judge Sotomayor argued that the court should not have reached the RFRA issue because it should have held that the ADEA does not apply to employment discrimination lawsuits by clergy members or other employees serving primarily religions roles. Instead, Judge Sotomayor would have avoided remand, deeming it a "wasteful expenditure of judicial resources and an unnecessary and uninvited burden on the parties."[101] Thus, she would have affirmed the district court's dismissal of the age discrimination claim.

As these cases indicate, there does not appear to be a particular pattern evident in Judge Sotomayor's civil rights opinions. Rather, the variety of outcomes suggests that her approach is reasonably balanced, given that she rejects some claims while accepting others, frequently agrees with her judicial colleagues, and rules both in favor of and against the party claiming discrimination. As a result, her opinions seem to betray neither a particular sympathy for nor hostility towards alleged victims of discrimination. If anything, Judge Sotomayor 's civil rights opinions appear to be rather workmanlike, in the sense that she appears to examine the evidence, apply precedent, and render a verdict without straying from established legal principles, actions that are not unusual given that many of the discrimination cases she has considered do not raise novel legal questions.

Civil Rights: Individuals with Disabilities[102]

Judge Sotomayor has written a number of decisions relating to the civil rights of individuals with disabilities under various federal statutes.[103] Many of her cases have related to the Americans with Disabilities Act (ADA),[104] which is a broad civil rights act that provides nondiscrimination protection for individuals with disabilities in many areas, including employment, public services, and public accommodation and services operated by private entities. She also has addressed discrimination issues which have arisen under Section 504 of the Rehabilitation Act,[105] which prohibits discrimination against an individual with a disability in a program or activity that receives federal financial assistance, an executive agency of the U.S. or the Postal Service,[106] as well as the Protection and Advocacy for Individuals with Mental Illness Act (PAIMI) [107] which ensures that "the rights of individuals with mental illness are protected."[108] Finally, Judge Sotomayor has decided a number of cases relating to the Individuals with Disabilities Education Act (IDEA),[109] which provides federal funding for the education of children with disabilities and requires, as a condition for the receipt of such funds, the provision of a free appropriate public education in the least restrictive environment.[110]

Judge Sotomayor 's decisions have been generally supportive of claims under these statutes, but she does not always rule in favor of plaintiffs with disabilities.[111] In her most discussed decision on disability issues, *Bartlett v. New York State Board of Bar Examiners*,[112] Judge Sotomayor appears to have anticipated the legislative discussions surrounding the enactment of the ADA Amendments Act[113] by finding that the use of self accommodations did not mean that the plaintiff was not an individual with a disability. In *Bartlett*, the plaintiff argued that she should be given reasonable accommodations when taking the New York bar exam because of her dyslexia. In evaluating whether the plaintiff was disabled, Judge Sotomayor observed that "[a] definition of disability based on outcomes alone, particularly in the context of learning disabilities, would prevent a court from finding a disability in the case of any individual like Dr. Bartlett who is extremely bright and hardworking, and who uses alternative routes to achieve academic success."[114] While analyzing the statutory and regulatory language, Judge Sotomayor also examined the implications of various legal arguments on the overall intent of the ADA.

Similarly, in *Connecticut Office of Protection and Advocacy for Persons with Disabilities v. Hartford Board of Education,*[115] Judge Sotomayor, writing for the court, addressed whether various federal statutes provided that the Connecticut Protection and Advocacy system should have access to a nonresidential school for children with serious emotional disturbances in order to investigate allegations of abuse and neglect. Finding that the system had such rights, Judge Sotomayor examined the purposes of the law to protect the legal and human rights of individuals with developmental disabilities and found that these purposes were not limited by the fact that a section of the act specifically provided authority to investigate certain incidents.

Judge Sotomayor 's opinions often turn on the particular facts presented. For example, in *Pell v. Columbia University*,[116] the facts surrounding the allegations of hostility to the plaintiff's dyslexia and the alleged discrimination regarding a foreign language requirement were closely examined. Similarly, in two fact-specific decisions regarding the application of the ADA's statute of limitations, Judge Sotomayor arrived at two different rulings.[117]

In her decisions, Judge Sotomayor examined the statutory language at issue,[118] as well as the applicable regulations and guidance[119] to inform her decisions. She also has relied upon the reasoning of other circuits in arriving at her decisions.[120] In the IDEA context, Judge Sotomayor has been described as "representative of the mainstream of prevailing judicial outcomes in K-12 education."[121]

ELECTION LAW[122]

During her tenure on the Second Circuit, Judge Sotomayor has not written extensively in the area of election law. Therefore, it is difficult to infer a great deal about her philosophy in the area. In a ballot access decision, she demonstrated careful consideration of the facts and a strong reliance on past precedent. Dissenting in a case involving the Voting Rights Act and felony disenfranchisement, her approach to statutory interpretation revealed an apparent preference for adhering to the plain meaning of the text, while simultaneously expressing deference to Congress.

Ballot Access

In *Rivera-Powell v. N.Y. City Board of Elections,*[123] the Second Circuit, affirming a district court decision, rejected a claim by a New York City judicial candidate alleging that violations of state law — removal of her name from the ballot based on alleged petition irregularities — resulted in deprivation of rights under the Fourteenth and First Amendments.[124] In rejecting these claims, Judge Sotomayor 's opinion demonstrated reliance on the facts presented, as well as on existing Second Circuit and Supreme Court case law, and the result was consistent with established precedents that court intervention in ordinary election disputes is inappropriate.

In analyzing the due process claim in *Rivera-Powell,* Judge Sotomayor 's opinion observed that judicial candidate Rivera-Powell received at least some type of pre-deprivation hearing, and that the record indicated that this hearing afforded her notice and the opportunity to be heard. The opinion further noted that analogous case law indicates that such a hearing comports with key requirements of due process.[125] Of greater importance, she determined that, subsequent to the Board's action, Rivera-Powell was given an opportunity for complete judicial review through a special proceeding under New York Election Law § 16-102 providing for expedited designation proceedings. According to Judge Sotomayor 's opinion, "[t]he combination of these two procedures satisfies due process."[126]

In rejecting the First Amendment claim, Judge Sotomayor's opinion found that it was "virtually indistinguishable" from Rivera-Powell's due process claim because she failed to allege additional and independent deprivation of interests.[127] Specifically, the opinion observed that Rivera-Powell did not challenge the state law requiring a certain number of signatures for ballot access or the law specifying requirements for objections, and that she did not contend that the Board of Elections' rules regarding submission of petitions or the filing of objections violated her rights in any respect. Instead, the opinion notes, she claimed that the Board applied these limitations illegally, burdening her right to participate in the electoral process. As a result, according to the opinion, her First Amendment claim was inextricably linked with the question of whether the state afforded her with procedurally adequate process.

Thus, Judge Sotomayor's opinion concluded: "[w]hen, as here, a plaintiff challenges a Board of Election decision not as stemming from a constitutionally or statutorily invalid law or regulation, but rather as contravening a law or regulation whose validity the plaintiff does not contest, there is no independent burden on First Amendment rights when the state provides adequate procedures by which to remedy the alleged illegality."[128] Cautioning that "a contrary holding would permit any plaintiff to obtain federal court review of even the most mundane election dispute merely by adding a First Amendment claim to his or her due process claim," the opinion concluded that it "would thereby undermine our holding – one which we share with many other circuits – that court intervention in 'garden variety' election disputes is inappropriate."[129]

Voting Rights Act and Felony Disenfranchisement

In *Hayden v. Pataki,*[130] an en banc Second Circuit decision, affirming the district court, rejected a challenge under Section 2 of the Voting Rights Act (VRA)[131] to a New York statute disenfranchising currently incarcerated felons and felons on parole. Section 2 of the VRA prohibits any voting qualification, standard, practice or procedure from being imposed by any state in a manner resulting in a denial or abridgement of the right of any citizen to vote on account of race or color. The court held that the VRA did not to cover felony disenfranchisement provisions because Congress did not intend or understand the VRA to encompass this type of statute, that such application of the VRA would alter the constitutional balance between the states and the federal government, and that Congress did not clearly indicate that it intended the VRA to alter the balance of government in such a manner. In addition to joining the main dissent from the en banc court decision, Judge Sotomayor also wrote separately, maintaining that the VRA applies to all voting qualifications, which include a state law disqualifying certain individuals from voting. Judge Sotomayor 's dissent, while arguably demonstrating a heavy reliance on the plain meaning of the statute, expresses deference to Congress.

In its decision, the Second Circuit characterized this case as presenting a "complex and difficult question" that, without congressional clarification, would require Supreme Court resolution.[132] It also noted that it has considered this question in the past without resolution, resulting in an evenly divided court.[133] In further support of its characterization of the issue, it pointed out that the Eleventh Circuit has ruled that the VRA does not encompass felony disenfranchisement, while the Ninth Circuit has found that it does.[134]

Beginning its analysis with a recitation of principles of statutory interpretation, the court noted that in interpreting a statute, the language of the statute itself must first be examined. If the statutory terms are unambiguous, the inquiry ends, and the statute is construed according to the plain meaning of its words. Relying on a Supreme Court case, *Robinson v. Shell Oil*,[135] the court acknowledged that the language of Section 2 is extremely broad, and without consideration of the larger context, could be interpreted to include felony disenfranchisement. Finding that there were persuasive reasons to conclude that Congress did not intend to include felony disenfranchisement within VRA coverage, the court decided that it must look beyond the plain meaning of the statute. In so doing, the court embarked upon a comprehensive analysis of congressional intent behind the VRA, its amendments, and subsequent election laws, concluding that Congress did not intend or understand the VRA to apply to felon disenfranchisement.

In sharp contrast to the majority decision, Judge Sotomayor, in a separate dissent written "to emphasize one point," disagreed that the issue under consideration was complex.[136] According to her dissent, "[i]t is plain to anyone reading the Voting Rights Act that it applies to all 'voting qualifications.'"[137] Further, she maintained that the New York felony disenfranchisement law clearly disqualifies a particular group of people from the right to vote. Therefore, Judge Sotomayor determined that the entire analysis in this case should have been limited only to those two propositions, and announced that it is "[t]he duty of a judge to follow the law, not to question its plain terms."[138] Congress does not want the courts to disregard the "plain language" of any statutory provision or to "invent exceptions" to its statutes, the judge admonished. Specifically criticizing the evidence presented by the majority opinion in support of its conclusion, Judge Sotomayor pointed out that the legislative history is void of even one Member of Congress expressly stating that felony disenfranchisement laws are beyond the reach of the VRA. Her dissent concluded that even if Congress doubted whether felony disenfranchisement laws should be subject to Section 2 of the VRA, "Congress would prefer to make any needed changes itself, rather than have courts do so for it."[139]

ABORTION[140]

During her tenure with the U.S. Court of Appeals for the Second Circuit, Judge Sotomayor has not addressed substantive legal questions involving abortion, such as the extent of the Constitution's protection of a woman's right to choose. Judge Sotomayor has, however, authored opinions that have examined the impact of foreign funding restrictions on domestic nonprofit organizations that promote abortion, and has discussed the effect of forced abortions and involuntary family planning practices in the context of applications for asylum. These opinions illustrate Judge Sotomayor's concern for precedent and her general adherence to established legal standards.

As discussed previously,[141] in *Center for Reproductive Law and Policy v. Bush*,[142] the Second Circuit considered an appeal brought by a nonprofit organization devoted to the promotion of reproductive rights. The Center for Reproductive Law and Policy ("CRLP") challenged the federal government's policy of conditioning the availability of U.S. government funds for foreign nongovernmental organizations on their agreement to neither perform nor promote abortion. CRLP argued that the so-called "Mexico City Policy" deprived the organization of its rights to freedom of speech and association under the First Amendment by limiting its interactions and communications with foreign nongovernmental organizations.[143] CRLP maintained that the Mexico City Policy discouraged foreign nongovernmental organizations from collaborating with it because the organizations feared being viewed as promoting abortion.

The Second Circuit affirmed the district court's dismissal of CRLP's claim on the grounds that the Mexico City Policy did not prohibit the organization from exercising its First Amendment rights. Writing for the court, Judge Sotomayor relied heavily on *Planned Parenthood Federation of America, Inc. v. Agency for International Development*,[144] a 1990 decision by the Second Circuit that also involved a First Amendment challenge to the Mexico City Policy by a domestic nonprofit organization. Judge Sotomayor explained: "*Planned Parenthood* not only controls this case conceptually; it presented the same issue. *Planned Parenthood* rejected the same First Amendment challenge to the same provision ... and no intervening Supreme Court case law alters its precedential value."[145]

While the district court dismissed CRLP's claim on the grounds that the organization lacked standing under Article III of the Constitution, the Second Circuit reached its decision after considering the merits of the claim and declining to resolve the standing question. After reviewing several decisions by the Supreme Court involving the assumption of standing by a court in order to proceed directly to the merits of a case, the Second Circuit reasoned that where a governmental provision is challenged as unconstitutional and another case has already entertained and rejected the same constitutional challenge to the same provision, a court may dispose of the case on the merits without addressing a novel question of jurisdiction.

Citing *Planned Parenthood*, the Second Circuit maintained that the Mexico City Policy did not implicate any constitutional rights. Domestic nonprofit organizations remained free to use their own funds to pursue abortion-related activities in foreign countries. The decision not to collaborate with CRLP because of the acceptance of U.S. government funds by a foreign nongovernmental organization had only an "incidental effect" on the activities of the CRLP that did not rise to the level of a constitutional violation.

In *Shi Liang Lin v. U.S. Dept. of Justice*,[146] the Second Circuit reviewed three orders issued by the Board of Immigration Appeals ("BIA") that denied applications for asylum submitted by three unmarried partners of individuals who were forced to have abortions in China. The BIA's denials were based on its conclusion that spouses of individuals who were forced to abort a pregnancy or submit to involuntary sterilization, but not the unmarried partners of such individuals, could automatically qualify for asylum as refugees under federal immigration law. In reviewing the BIA's orders, the Second Circuit sought to determine whether § 601(a) of the Illegal Immigration Reform and Immigrant Responsibility Act of 1996, which amended the definition for the term "refugee" to include individuals who were forced to abort a pregnancy or submit to involuntary sterilization, was ambiguous, so that the BIA's construction of the term was entitled to deference.

The Second Circuit evaluated the BIA's interpretation of §601(a) in accordance with the principles articulated by the Supreme Court in *Chevron U.S.A. v. NRDC*. In *Chevron*, the Suprme Court established a two-part test for determining when an agency's interpretation of a statute that it administers is entitled to deference. First, a reviewing court will consider whether Congress has spoken on the question at issue. If the intent of Congress is clear, the court must "give effect to the unambiguously expressed intent of Congress." If the statute is silent or ambiguous, however, a court will examine whether the agency's interpretation constitutes a permissible construction of the statute.

The Second Circuit, however, not only held that unmarried partners of persons who were threatened with forced abortion or involuntary sterilization were not entitled to asylum, but that the BIA's interpretation of § 601(a) extending such protections to spouses was also unfounded. The court held that Congress had spoken unambiguously about who may be deemed a refugee for purposes of asylum eligibility, and that nothing in the definition of the term "refugee" permits a person to obtain asylum if he or she has not personally experienced persecution or a well-rounded fear of future persecution. It explained:

> We do not deny that an individual whose spouse undergoes, or is threatened with, a forced abortion or involuntary sterilization may suffer a profound emotional loss as a partner and a potential parent. But such a loss does not change the requirement that we must follow the "ordinary meaning" of the language chosen by Congress, according to which an individual does not automatically qualify for "refugee" status on account of a coercive procedure performed on someone else.[147]

Thus, the Second Circuit maintained that § 601(a) seemed to deny asylum protection to the spouses of individuals forced to abort a pregnancy or submit to involuntary sterilization, as well as the unmarried partners of such individuals.

In a concurring opinion, Judge Sotomayor criticized the majority opinion for its lack of judicial restraint. In response to the majority's conclusion that even spouses of individuals forced to abort a pregnancy or submit to involuntary sterilization may not be automatically eligible for asylum, Judge Sotomayor noted:

> Instead of answering the limited question before us – whether the BIA's denial of asylum to the unmarried partners of women forced to undergo abortions or sterilization was unreasonable – the majority has chosen to go beyond it to address an issue that is unbriefed, unargued, and unnecessary to resolve this appeal.[148]

Judge Sotomayor noted that because Congress did not indicate how direct the harm or injury must be before it can be determined that an individual suffers persecution and should be considered a "refugee" for purposes of asylum protection, the BIA's construction of the term should be entitled to deference so long as it is reasonable. Judge Sotomayor maintained that the majority opinion failed to explain why the harm of forced abortion or sterilization constituted persecution only for the person undergoing the procedure and not for the spouse. Forced abortion, Judge Sotomayor observed, could be devastating for the spouse, as well as the woman:

> The termination of a wanted pregnancy under a coercive population control program can only be devastating to any couple, akin, no doubt, to the killing of a child ... In the end, I fail to understand how the majority can claim that the harm caused by a spouse's forced abortion or sterilization is not a personal harm to

> both spouses – either or both of whom can be sterilized for violations of the population control programs – especially given the unique biological nature of pregnancy and special reverence every civilization has accorded to child- rearing and parenthood in marriage.[149]

In *Zheng v. Gonzales*,[150] the Second Circuit reviewed a BIA order that dismissed an appeal by a woman seeking asylum based on the involuntary insertion of an intrauterine device ("IUD"). The immigration judge that first considered the petitioner's case denied her application for asylum on the grounds that IUD implantation did not constitute persecution and that "Congress did not intend to include birth control methods other than abortion or forced sterilization in its definition of persecution.... "[151] The BIA agreed with the immigration judge and noted that Zheng had not been persecuted, in part, because she did not experience a "significant degree of pain or restriction as a result of the procedure."[152] The BIA also acknowledged the widespread use of IUDs as a method of birth control and observed that there is nothing so inherently egregious about the procedure to conclude that Zheng was persecuted.

Judge Sotomayor, writing for the court, remanded the case to the BIA "so that it might articulate its position concerning whether and under what conditions the forced insertion of an IUD constitutes persecution."[153] The BIA had taken contrary positions on whether the involuntary insertion of an IUD constituted persecution, finding in at least one other case that such insertion was persecution. Judge Sotomayor also noted that the BIA had not discussed the issue in a published, precedential opinion. The BIA's failure to explain when the involuntary insertion of an IUD would constitute persecution "deprive[d] the bench, the bar and potential asylum applicants of guidance concerning whether and how they might approach the issue."[154]

FREEDOM OF INFORMATION ACT[155]

During her 11 years as a federal appellate judge, Judge Sotomayor has authored two opinions involving the Freedom of Information Act (FOIA).[156] Both of the FOIA decisions – *Tigue v. Department of Justice* and *Wood v. Federal Bureau of Investigation* – upheld the withholding of requested records by the government. Because the opinions are few and relied on relevant Supreme Court precedent, it is difficult to draw conclusions from them regarding her overall approach to FOIA or to related matters such as individual privacy or transparency in government.

FOIA applies to records held by agencies of the executive branch of the federal government.[157] With the exception of three special law enforcement exclusions and records already made available for publication or inspection, all other federal agency records may be requested under the FOIA. Agencies are required to make records not subject to a FOIA exemption available upon request. Nine categories of information may be exempted from FOIA disclosure.[158] Judge Sotomayor 's opinions primarily involved exemptions 5 and 6—regarding inter- and intra-agency memoranda and disclosures which would invade personal privacy, respectively. In both opinions, Judge Sotomayor noted that the Supreme Court has mandated that FOIA's exemptions are to be construed narrowly.

Exemption 5

FOIA's Exemption 5 applies to "inter-agency or intra-agency memorandums or letters which would not be made available by law to a party other than an agency in litigation with the agency."[159] In the two Second Circuit FOIA opinions authored by Judge Sotomayor, the court examined the scope and application of two privileges incorporated into FOIA Exemption 5 – the deliberative process privilege and the attorney work-product privilege. The deliberative process privilege protects advice, recommendations, and opinions from disclosure. The rationale behind the privilege is to promote candid and frank discussion in agency deliberations, to protect against premature disclosure of agency deliberations, and to ensure that agencies are judged only by their final decisions.[160] The attorney work-product privilege protects documents prepared by an attorney for litigation that reflect her theory of the case or litigation strategy.

In *Tigue v. Department of Justice,*[161] the Second Circuit held that a memorandum prepared by an Assistant United States Attorney for a commission tasked by the IRS with conducting a review of the IRS's Criminal Investigations Department was an "inter-agency" communication protected by the deliberative process privilege and thus properly withheld under FOIA Exemption 5. In concluding that the privilege applied, Judge Sotomayor wrote that although the Commission was not an "agency" in the traditional sense, the entity acted as a consultant to (i.e. an agent of) the IRS. Consequently, the memorandum was properly considered to be an inter-agency communication between the U.S. Attorney's office and the IRS. Her opinion considered the court's conclusion in light of the Supreme Court's decision in *Department of the Interior v. Klamath Water Users Protective Ass'n,*[162] where the Court found that correspondence between an Indian Tribe and the Bureau of Indian Affairs was not exempt from disclosure as inter-agency or intra-agency communication. Unlike the Klamath Tribe, which advocated its own positions in the judicial proceedings, the Second Circuit found that the commission was more akin to the agency's own personnel in that it was not representing its own interest, but that of the IRS.

Because the memorandum was specifically prepared for use by the commission in assisting the IRS in its future decision making, the court held that the document fell within the pre-decisional prong of Exemption 5.[163] It also rejected the argument that the memorandum lost its privileged status because it was incorporated by reference in the commission's report to the IRS. As delineated in a Supreme Court case, *NLRB v. Sears, Roebuck & Co.,* an agency may be required to disclose a document otherwise entitled to protection if the agency has expressly adopted or incorporated the document by reference in a final opinion.[164] Applying *Sears*, Judge Sotomayor concluded that minor references[165] in the Report to the Memo were not an adoption or incorporation in a final opinion and did not result in the government's waiver of the deliberative process privilege.[166] Moreover, she noted that the memorandum was not a "final opinion" because the report was not written by IRS officials.

In *Wood v. Federal Bureau of Investigation*,[167] discussed below, the Second Circuit, in an opinion written by Judge Sotomayor, similarly held that a prosecution memorandum fell within the attorney work-product privilege and thus was properly withheld under Exemption 5.

Exemption 6

Exemption 6 of FOIA protects from disclosure "personnel and medical files and similar files the disclosure of which would result in a clearly unwarranted invasion of personal privacy."[168] As delineated in a Supreme Court case, *Department of State v. Washington Post Co.*,[169] the term "similar files" has "a broad, rather than narrow, meaning" and applies to "detailed government records on an individual which can be identified as applying to that individual."[170] In addition, the determination of Exemption 6's applicability entails a "balancing of private against public interests" rather than an examination of "the nature of the files."[171]

In *Wood*,[172] the Second Circuit evaluated whether Exemption 6 protected documents containing the names of government investigators in an internal FBI probe. Writing for the court, Judge Sotomayor employed a two-part test, first determining whether the information is contained in a file "similar" to a medical or personnel file,[173] and then balancing the public's need for the information against the individual's privacy interest to determine whether the disclosure of names would constitute a clearly unwarranted invasion of personal privacy.[174] With regard to whether the files at issue were "similar" to medical or personnel files, the court found that personnel and medical files contain information about a person, and that administrative investigative files were also likely to contain information about the subject of the investigation and third parties such as witnesses.[175] The court held that any personal information, not limited to information about the subject of an investigation, contained in files similar to personnel or medical files is subject to the balancing analysis under Exemption 6. It then balanced the investigators "broad" privacy interest against possible harassment and embarrassment against the public's interest in information that would shed light on an agency's performance of its duties. Judge Sotomayor's opinion concluded that the public's interest in knowing the identity of the investigators was minimal at best because it would add little to the public's understanding of how the agency performed its duties. Thus, it was insufficient to overcome the employees' substantial interest in preventing public disclosure of their names.

CRIMINAL LAW[176]

Based to some extent on her opinions in Fourth Amendment cases – in particular on two opinions she has written in cases involving the typical remedy for Fourth Amendment violations, the so- called "exclusionary rule" – some commentators have speculated that Judge Sotomayor would be more likely to rule in favor of police or prosecutors in criminal cases than was Justice Souter.[177] However, it is difficult to glean any strong evidence of such an inclination from her appellate court opinions. She has authored several opinions in the criminal law area, and joined others, in which the Second Circuit ruled in favor of the police or government. On the other hand, she has authored opinions on behalf of the court that reach the opposite outcome. In addition, in cases in which Judge Sotomayor has split with her panel colleagues to write a dissenting opinion, her arguments have generally favored defendants. More than any other unifying characteristic, her appellate opinions in the criminal justice area, as in many other areas, demonstrate her strong adherence to precedent.

Fourth Amendment

The Fourth Amendment to the U.S. Constitution provides a right "of the people to be secure in their persons, houses, papers, and effects, against unreasonable searches and seizures."[178] The reasonableness inquiry is prompted when government either conducts a "search" by invading a person's "reasonable expectation of privacy" or conducts a "seizure" by "meaningfully interfering" with a person's possessory interest or freedom of movement. [179] As a general rule, reasonableness requires "probable cause" and either a warrant or a warrant exception.[180] However, in some circumstances, for example when the government demonstrates a "special need," courts conduct a "reasonableness balancing" inquiry rather than requiring probable cause.

During her tenure on the Second Circuit, Judge Sotomayor has written several opinions in cases with Fourth Amendment implications. Most, if not all, of these concern the reasonableness of a search or seizure, but some address additional questions such as whether evidence collected pursuant to a Fourth Amendment violation must be excluded at trial.

Reasonableness of a Search or Seizure

In *United States v. Gori*[181] and *N. G. ex rel. S.C. v. Connecticut,*[182] Judge Sotomayor wrote dissenting opinions in which she argued for a stronger protection from unreasonable searches and seizures than the majority opinion allowed. In *Gori*, police officers suspected, based on an informant's tips, that an apartment might contain evidence of drugs. Relying on that evidence, they stood on either side of a food delivery person, who happened to be making a delivery to the apartment, as she knocked on the apartment door. After the door opened, the officers announced their presence and ordered all of the apartment's occupants into the hallway. The officers questioned the occupants, obtained signatures on consent forms, and completed a full search of the apartment. At issue on appeal of the subsequent conviction was whether a Supreme Court case, *Payton v. New York,*[183] applied. Stating that "the Fourth Amendment has drawn a firm line at the entrance to the house," *Payton* established a heightened standard that police officer's must meet in order to enter a home. [184] Applying another Supreme Court case, *Santana v. United States,*[185] the majority held that because the apartment occupants had opened the door and exposed the apartment interior to the officers, they lacked a reasonable expectation of privacy and thus the Fourth Amendment warrant requirement, and the heightened *Payton* standard, did not apply. In dissent, Judge Sotomayor argued that the majority had misapplied *Santana* and that the heightened protection should have applied under *Payton*. In having argued for special protection for the home, Judge Sotomayor stated that "I agree [with Scalia's view, articulated in *Arizona v. Hicks*, 480 U.S. 321, 329 (1987)] that the Fourth Amendment's protection of the home is worth ... preservation."[186]

In *N. G. ex rel. S.C.* ,[187] a case involving strip searches of adolescent girls in a juvenile detention facility, Judge Sotomayor dissented from the part of the majority opinion which had upheld the strip searches. In upholding the searches, the majority had relied on the "special needs" doctrine, under which a search or seizure is subject to a balancing test rather than the ordinary probable cause or warrant requirements. The doctrine applies when the government has articulated a "special nee[d], beyond the normal need for law enforcement, [made] the warrant and probable cause requirements impracticable."[188] Although she agreed that the government had a special need to search girls in the facility, she disagreed that the strip search method, in particular, bore a sufficiently "close and substantial" relationship to the government's special need. [189]

In contrast, Judge Sotomayor authored opinions in several cases in which the Second Circuit held that a government search was reasonable and thus did not violate the Fourth Amendment. In *Leventhal v. Knapek*,[190] the New York State Department of Transportation had searched one of its employee's computers as part of an investigation of employee misconduct. Writing for the court, Judge Sotomayor noted that governments must abide by the Fourth Amendment prohibition against unreasonable searches and seizures even in their role as employers.[191] However, she applied a Supreme Court precedent, *O'Connor v. Ortega*,[192] to hold that although the employee had a reasonable expectation of privacy in the contents of his office computer, the government's search was not unreasonable because it was both "'justified at its inception' and of appropriate scope," specifically because the Department had various indications that the employee had been misusing his work computer. [193]

In *Cassidy v. Chertoff*, [194] also discussed previously,[195] Judge Sotomayor demonstrated a deference to government in the national security context. Pursuant to legislation enacted after the 9/11 terrorist attacks,[196] the U.S. Coast Guard required specified vessels to undertake various security measures, including, in some cases, the screening of passengers' vehicles or bags. The plaintiffs in *Cassidy* were two Vermont residents who regularly commuted on a ferry which had imposed searches on passengers' belongings pursuant to the statute. Despite alleging that they feared repercussions if they did not acquiesce in the searches, the plaintiffs sued, seeking a declaratory judgment and an injunction preventing the searches. Writing for the court, Judge Sotomayor applied the special needs doctrine. After a thorough discussion of the various interests involved, she concluded that the government's interest in the searches outweighed the intrusion on the plaintiffs' privacy.

Finally, in an opinion written by Sotomayor in a 2007 case, *United States v. Howard*, the Second Circuit held that the warrantless search of a defendant's automobile was not a Fourth Amendment violation because the police had established probable cause to support the search based on six phone calls in which cocaine was discussed. [197]

Exclusionary Rule

The "exclusionary rule" is a remedy for violations of the Fourth Amendment prohibition against unreasonable searches and seizures. To deter Fourth Amendment violations, the rule requires courts to forbid the prosecution's use of evidence obtained as a result of an unconstitutional search or seizure.[198] http://apps.crs.gov/products/r/html/R40 1 89.html - fn1 0

In *United States v. Leon*,[199] the Supreme Court introduced what has come to be known as the good-faith exception to the exclusionary rule. Under *Leon*, the exclusionary rule does not apply when police officers act with "objectively reasonable reliance" on a search warrant later found to be invalid. Subsequently, in *Arizona v. Evans*,[200] the Supreme Court applied *Leon* to evidence obtained after an arrest based on a facially valid warrant that the clerk of the court had neglected to show had been quashed seventeen days earlier.

Judge Sotomayor authored two opinions – *United States v. Santa* and *United States v. Falso* – as an appellate judge which some commentators have characterized as having extended precedents that narrowed the scope of the exclusionary rule by expanding the *Leon* good-faith exception.[201] In both cases, she applied Supreme Court precedent to hold that the rule was inapplicable, thus allowing the convictions to stand. However, although the outcomes favored the prosecutors in both cases, Judge Sotomayor 's opinions relied on, but arguably did not extend, relevant Supreme Court precedents.[202]

Judge Sotomayor most recently applied the good-faith exception in *United States v. Falso*.[203] In *Falso*, FBI officers obtained a warrant to search David Falso's home after connecting a login name used to access a website containing child pornography with Falso's *Yahoo!* account. Writing for the court, Judge Sotomayor held, first, that the search warrant had been granted without sufficient probable cause. Nonetheless, she then applied the good-faith exception to the exclusionary rule to allow the prosecution's use of the evidence. The two other

Second Circuit judges sitting on the panel each joined with one part of this opinion. In the first part of the opinion, Judge Sotomayor distinguished this case from a prior Second Circuit case, *United States v. Martin*,[204] in which the court had held that a defendant's membership in a website containing child pornography was sufficient to establish probable cause to justify a warrant for a search. Unlike in *Martin*, Judge Sotomayor wrote, there was no solid evidence that Falso had even accessed the site, much less that he had actually downloaded pornographic images. Thus, the court held that the warrant was invalid and the search constituted a Fourth Amendment violation. The second part of the opinion held that the evidence found during the search could nonetheless be used to convict Falso because the officers who obtained the warrant had acted in good faith. Applying *Leon*, Judge Sotomayor noted that the officers had not misled the issuing court, nor had the affidavit supporting the warrant been obviously deficient.

In an earlier case, *United States v. Santa*,[205] a police officer from Spring Valley, New York, arrested Anthony Santa, a man whom the officer recognized as having "been the subject of previous criminal investigations."[206] The officer made the arrest after learning from a dispatcher that an outstanding arrest warrant from a neighboring town applied to Santa. In a search of Santa's person subsequent to the arrest, the officer found plastic bags filled with crack cocaine. However, the arrest warrant upon which the officer had relied was supposed to have been vacated; the issuing court had mistakenly misdirected its request to vacate to the wrong police department. Thus, when he made the arrest, the officer had neither a valid arrest warrant nor probable cause to suspect that Santa had committed a crime. In such circumstances, the Fourth Amendment violation is apparent; the remaining question is whether the exclusionary rule should bar the prosecution's use of the evidence. http://apps.crs.gov/products/r/html/R40189.html-fn26 Writing for the court in *Santa*, Judge Sotomayor held that under *Evans*, the exclusionary rule could not bar the evidence seized.

Commentators have drawn analogies between Judge Sotomayor's rationale in *Santa* and a 2009 Supreme Court case, *United States v. Herring*,[207] in which the Supreme Court's five more conservative justices joined to narrow the exclusionary rule. However, the analogies are arguably misplaced. Although *Herring* involved factual circumstances that are remarkably similar to those in *Santa* in many respects, a key distinction – namely that the record error in *Herring* was committed by police officers themselves rather than by a court employee – distinguishes the two cases. In other words, whereas the holding in *Santa* represents an application of the good-faith exception as interpreted in *Evans*, *Herring* was an extension of that exception. To support the court's holding in

Santa, Judge Sotomayor's opinion emphasizes the distinction between judicial errors, which were at issue in *Evans* and *Santa*, and police errors. This emphasis mirrors points made by Justice Breyer in his dissenting opinion in *Herring*. Both Judge Sotomayor and Justice Breyer 's opinions highlighted the substantive distinction between errors made by judicial branch personnel and errors made by police, noting three specific distinctions that the *Evans* court had emphasized, namely: (1) the exclusionary rule historically aims to deter police, rather than judicial, misconduct; (2) no evidence suggests that court employees are "inclined to subvert the Fourth Amendment"; and (3) because judicial officers have no stake in the outcome of particular criminal investigations, "there [is] 'no basis for believing that application of the exclusionary rule ... [would] have a significant effect on court employees.'"[208]

Based on these few cases, it is difficult to determine what approach Judge Sotomayor would take to the Fourth Amendment exclusionary rule as a Supreme Court justice. On one hand, she appears to apply exclusionary rule precedents that are perceived as conservative without attempting to narrow the precedents. On the other hand, this respect for precedent appears to be in keeping with her more general respect for *stare decisis*.

Police Immunity

While serving on the Second Circuit, Judge Sotomayor has authored opinions in several police immunity cases. A number of these arose in the context of suits for civil damages brought by plaintiffs who alleged that police officers violated the Fourth Amendment or another constitutional guarantee and should be liable for civil damages under 42 U.S.C. § 1983.[209]

Notwithstanding the cause of action provided by § 1983, police officers are immune from liability in civil suits if "their conduct does not violate clearly established statutory or constitutional rights of which a reasonable person would have known."[210] The most difficult police immunity cases turn on an analysis of whether a given constitutional guarantee is "clearly established."

The Second Circuit held that police officers were entitled to immunity in several cases in which Judge Sotomayor authored the opinion for a unanimous Second Circuit panel. In *Smith v. Edwards*,[211] John Smith brought a § 1983 claim for false arrest after he was arrested in connection with allegations that he had sexually abused his three-year-old daughter. Although the police officer had arrested Smith pursuant to a warrant, Smith claimed that the warrant was invalid due to a "material omission" because in the affidavit to the issuing magistrate, the officer had included incriminating allegations of sexual abuse but neglected to include relevant proceedings, including the denial of a protective order, in a lower court. Writing for the court, Judge Sotomayor applied a Second Circuit precedent under which such an omission is material if inclusion of the omitted material would have undermined probable cause.[212] She examined the relevant lower court proceedings, which appeared to raise some questions regarding statements made by Smith's wife and daughter, but did not come to any ultimate conclusion regarding the legitimacy of the allegations. Given these facts, Judge Sotomayor concluded that Smith's § 1983 claim must fail because "nothing in the [omitted] proceedings would have negated probable cause."[213]

In another case evaluating probable cause in light of a § 1983 claim, *Anthony v. City of New York*,[214] police responded to a 911 call in which a caller, identified by the 911 operator as being potentially emotionally disturbed, had stated that her husband beat her and had a knife and a gun. The manner in which the officers gained entry is unclear, but once inside the home, they found Myra Anthony, a woman with Downs syndrome, home alone. The officers transported Anthony to a county hospital, where she stayed overnight and was subject to psychological evaluations. After the incident, Anthony and her guardian, Magdalene Wright, sued the officers under §1983, claiming damages arising from Fourth Amendment violations. Writing for the court, Judge Sotomayor first noted Second Circuit and other circuits' precedent under which "[a] warrantless seizure for the purpose of involuntary hospitalization 'may be made only upon probable case, that is, only if there are reasonable grounds for believing that the person seized' is dangerous to herself or to others."[215] Applying that standard to the facts in the case, the court held that the officers were entitled to qualified immunity because the emotional 911 call prompting the officers' entry appeared to provide reasonable grounds to believe that Anthony was dangerous.

In *Rolon v. Henneman*, the court considered whether a police officer who testified in a discretionary hearing has absolute immunity from civil suit for actions related to the testimony.[216] The plaintiff argued that the officer's testimony had caused humiliation and economic loss. Writing for the court, Judge Sotomayor noted that the alleged injuries did not constitute a cognizable deprivation of liberty or property. Although the opinion focused on fact-specific circumstances (for example, the court found that the plaintiff had not demonstrated that he had lost overtime work as a result of the testimony), the holding extends a Supreme Court case, *Briscoe v. LaHue*,[217] in which the Court had held that officers are entitled to absolute immunity for actions arising from mandatory testimony.

In a few other cases, Judge Sotomayor authored opinions in which the Second Circuit denied immunity for at least some actions. In *Walczyk v. Rio*,[218] Thomas Walczyk and several of his family members sued the members of the police department in their Connecticut town, claiming civil damages arising from the police officers' alleged Fourth Amendment violations in connection with the search of Walczyk's home, his mother's home and Walczyk's arrest. The Second Circuit held that the police were entitled to immunity for damages arising from the search of Walcyzk's home and for his arrest, both of which it found to be supported by probable cause and therefore not prohibited by the Fourth Amendment. However, it held that the police were not entitled to qualified immunity with respect to the search of Walczyk's mother's home because the police had based the search on "stale information."[219] In a concurring opinion, Judge Sotomayor agreed with the outcome, but disagreed with some elements of the court's reasoning. Namely, in analyzing the immunity question, the majority opinion had first analyzed whether the Fourth Amendment right at issue was "clearly established" and next examined whether a "reasonable officer" would be aware of the right. Judge Sotomayor expressed concern that this two-step approach had "bifurcate[d] the 'clearly established' inquiry" in contravention of settled Supreme Court precedent.[220] Her concerns appeared to be aimed at adhering to precedent and at not complicating the test for future qualified immunity cases. In addition, she urged the court to resist widening the established limits of qualified immunity, emphasizing that the court's approach might give police officers "a second bite at the immunity the apple."[221]

Judge Sotomayor 's police immunity opinion that is least favorable to police officers is *Papineau v. Parmley*, a case involving a break up of a protest demonstration by members of the Onondaga Nation.[222] The demonstration was prompted by an agreement between New York State and the Onondaga Nation to impose a state tax on some tobacco purchases made on the Onondaga reservation. The demonstration proceeded with the knowledge of county police and without incident for several days, but state police officers became involved when some protesters entered an interstate highway. Although the protesters left the highway peacefully at the request of one of the demonstration leaders, state police marched toward the place where the protesters had gathered, about 70 feet from the highway. The officers then received a "go ahead" order from a police major who was located out of view of the protesters. The state police then "charged into the demonstration and began arresting protesters allegedly indiscriminately, assaulting [protesters], beating them with their riot batons, dragging them by their hair and kicking them."[223] The demonstrators brought a § 1983 claim, alleging violations of their First and Fourth Amendment rights. Regarding the Fourth

Amendment claim, Judge Sotomayor's opinion noted that as delineated in a Supreme Court case, *Grahm v. Connor*,[224] police force is excessive if it is unreasonable given all of the circumstances. Given the circumstances in this case, including the peaceful nature of many demonstrators, the court concluded that, as a matter of law, the police officers would not be entitled to qualified immunity.

Sixth Amendment and *Habeas Corpus*

During her tenure on the appellate bench, Judge Sotomayor has authored opinions in several cases involving writs of *habeas corpus*. Her *habeas* opinions involve various aspects of Sixth Amendment law such as jury selection, the right to counsel and ineffective assistance of counsel. Few of these decisions have garnered a dissent. As in other areas, Judge Sotomayor has relied on Supreme Court and Second Circuit precedent in opinions addressing *habeas* and the Sixth Amendment. In addition, the opinions demonstrate a recognition of the Sixth Amendment's import and a willingness to provide defendants with a right to appeal.

Many *habeas* cases require federal courts to evaluate decisions made by state courts. However, under the "deference" provision of the Antiterrorism and Effective Death Penalty Act of 1996 (AEDPA),[225] federal courts may not overturn state judgments by granting a *habeas* writ merely because they would have decided the case differently from the state court. They may overturn only state decisions contrary to Supreme Court precedent or applied unreasonably.[226] Within the broad zone in which reasonable judges may differ, state court decisions typically stand. In applying these general *habeas* parameters, the Second Circuit has deferred to state court decisions in some, but not all, instances.[227]

Jury Selection

In a 2001 case, *Galarza v. Keane*,[228] the principal issue involved application of the Supreme Court precedent in *Batson v. Kentucky*[229] regarding peremptory challenges to potential jurors during the jury selection process. In *Galarza*, the prosecutors peremptorily struck a number of Hispanic jurors, leading the defendant's counsel to raise a *Batson* challenge. As required by *Batson*, the trial judge required the prosecution to articulate a non-racial basis for the strikes. The defense counsel objected to the explanations as pretextual. While the judge specifically declared that he credited the prosecution's explanations with respect to some of the prospective jurors, the court made no clear finding with respect to the others. However, the trial judge permitted all of the strikes to stand. At that time, the defense counsel did not object to the court's failure to specifically declare whether he credited the prosecution's explanations with respect to some of the prospective jurors. After the jury found Galarza guilty of numerous narcotic offenses, he appealed his conviction on equal protection grounds, alleging that the prosecutor exercised her peremptory challenges in a racially discriminatory manner.

Judge Sotomayor, writing for the majority,[230] found that the trial court failed to fulfill its obligations under *Batson* as to some of the prospective jurors. Although the majority deferred to the trial court's findings regarding two of the prospective jurors, it found the trial court's record deficient as to findings regarding three other challenges. In addition, Judge Sotomayor's opinion rejected the prosecution's assertion that by failing to make an appropriate objection, for several reasons the defendant was procedurally barred from raising his *Batson* claim in federal court. First, it concluded that the state court had not relied on the defendant's failure as a ground for denying his *Batson* claim on direct or state *habeas* review. Second, it applied Second Circuit precedent under which a procedural failure in a trial is not a bar to federal *habeas* relief unless the state courts rely on the failure to deny relief. Third, in a relatively less restrictive reading of *Batson*, Judge Sotomayor wrote that "we decline to create a procedural requirement that a party must repeat his or her *Batson* challenge three times at trial in order to avoid a procedural bar."[231] For these reasons, the court vacated the district court's denial of Galarza's *habeas* petition and remanded the case to the district court to address the *Batson* claims.

Right to Counsel

In *Gilchrist v. O 'Keefe*,[232] the Second Circuit rejected an inmate's claim that he was unconstitutionally deprived of his right to counsel during his state sentencing proceeding. Shortly before sentencing, the trial judge declined to appoint a new attorney after previous counsel withdrew from the case because the defendant had punched him in the ear and ruptured his eardrum. The defendant appeared without counsel at sentencing and received a sentence of 48 to 144 months. The defendant subsequently filed a petition for a writ of *habeas corpus*, alleging that his Sixth Amendment right to counsel had been violated.

In an opinion authored by Judge Sotomayor, despite noting that it would have preferred a different handling of the situation, the court held that the state court had acted in a manner consistent with Supreme Court precedent. In reaching its conclusion, the court addressed three issues. First, it determined whether Supreme Court precedent recognized a distinction between a waiver (requiring a warning as the defendant alleged) and forfeiture (as the state alleged) of constitutional rights. Second, it addressed which Supreme Court precedent would govern any such distinction. Finally, it considered whether the state court's action was consistent with such precedent.

Relying on Supreme Court precedent, Judge Sotomayor wrote that "even absent a warning, a defendant may be found to have forfeited certain trial-related constitutional rights based on certain types of misconduct."[233] In addition, her opinion concluded that Supreme Court precedent recognizes a distinction between a waiver and a forfeiture of constitutional rights. However, it noted that there is no Supreme Court precedent specifically addressing forfeiture of the right to counsel. In the absence of such precedent, the majority concluded that the state court rulings were not contrary to clearly established federal law.

In determining whether the state court's holding constituted an unreasonable application of the law, the majority looked to other circuits and concluded that sister circuits extended Supreme Court precedent to the Sixth Amendment right to counsel. Finding these conclusions unpersuasive, the court held that the trial court's ruling was a reasonable application. However, it noted that its holding was narrow, applying only to the *habeas* standard and not to the larger question of the constitutionality of the denial of the right to counsel under these circumstances. In addition, it noted that in light of the importance of the Sixth Amendment right to counsel, trial courts should exercise other means instead of denying a defendant the right.

In *Campusano v. United States*,[234] a criminal defendant argued that he had suffered *per se* ineffective assistance of counsel because his attorney had failed to file a notice of appeal. The defendant had twice instructed the attorney to file the appeal and the attorney had neglected to do so. However, the defendant's plea agreement contained a provision stipulating that he would not appeal or otherwise challenge his sentence provided the sentence fell within a stipulated range of 108-135 months, and he had been sentenced to 108 months. The defendant subsequently filed a *habeas* claim to vacate, set aside or correct his sentence on the basis of ineffective assistance of counsel. He argued that the failure to file a requested notice of appeal constituted ineffective assistance and that no independent showing of prejudice was required.

In an opinion by Judge Sotomayor, the court held that even after a waiver, an attorney who believes that the requested appeal would be frivolous is bound to comply with the client's wishes and file the notice of appeal by submitting an *Anders*[235] brief. Failure to do so, she wrote, satisfies the presumption of prejudice required by a Supreme Court case, *Roe v. Flores-Ortega.*[236] She also noted that while plea waivers were enforceable in most cases, "important constitutional rights require some exceptions to the presumptive enforceability of a waiver,"[237] and these rights are endangered when an attorney fails to file a notice of appeal. Thus, the court remanded the case to the district court for a determination of whether Campusano in fact did instruct his attorney to file an appeal.

INTERNATIONAL ISSUES[238]

Among circuit court opinions written by Judge Sotomayor having international implications are a dissent involving the Hague Convention on the Civil Aspects of International Child Abduction, a dissent involving federal alienage jurisdiction, and two opinions for the court involving a civil RICO suit brought by foreign governments claiming that defendant tobacco companies sought to avoid paying foreign taxes by smuggling cigarettes into plaintiffs' territory. Whereas Judge Sotomayor's dissent regarding the interpretation of the Hague Convention remains a minority rule in federal courts, her broad approach to alienage jurisdiction where firms of overseas territories are involved, an approach widely adopted by federal courts, was later approved by the Supreme Court and also became the rule in the Second Circuit. Her decision that the revenue rule barred the civil RICO case brought by the European Communities and other governments against various tobacco manufacturers, a ruling based on Second Circuit precedent that the Supreme Court had declined to review, was remanded by the Court in light of an intervening ruling that the revenue rule did not apply to a government prosecution under a different statute. She reinstated the court's original decision finding that it was not called into question by the Supreme Court case, a judgment the Court also let stand.

Together, the dissenting opinions show an inclination on the part of Judge Sotomayor to bring an international perspective to her analysis, reading the Convention as protecting parental rights adversely affected by cross-border actions by other parents and looking at the jurisdictional statute in light of how the majority's narrow interpretation and its resulting denial of a neutral judicial forum for disputes with international implications would affect U.S. commercial relations with other countries. Judge Sotomayer also consulted and analyzed foreign case law in the Hague Convention case, but viewed this task as instructional rather than necessary to forming her conclusion. Judge Sotomayor 's opinions on the application of the revenue rule, which in following Second Circuit precedent continued to make the circuit unavailable as a forum for foreign government plaintiffs, took foreign policy considerations into account at length. Because separation of powers concerns were a key factor in why the revenue rule was applied, however, she found that the conduct of foreign relations was best left to the political branches and refrained from allowing the litigation to continue in the absence of clear signals from the branches that they intended such cases to proceed.

Hague Child Abduction Convention

Croll v. Croll,[239] a case of first impression for the Second Circuit, required the court to interpret the widely ratified Hague Convention on the Civil Aspects of International Child Abduction. The case involved an issue that remains unsettled under U.S. law and internationally, that is, whether a parent's right of access coupled with a *ne exeat* clause, i.e., a clause in a custody order prohibiting the custodial parent from removing a child from a certain location, conferred a right of custody, thus permitting the non-custodial parent to exercise a right of return under the Convention. Reversing the district court, the Second Circuit ruled 2-1 that "a *ne exeat* clause does not transmute access rights into rights of custody under the Convention" and ultimately that the district court lacked jurisdiction to order the child's return to Hong Kong, as requested by the child's father. In a dissenting opinion, Judge Sotomayor opined that the *ne exeat* clause granted joint rights of custody to the father and the Hong Kong court that had issued the original custody order and would have affirmed the district court's decision. The Supreme Court denied certioriari.

The Hague Convention has as its objects "to secure the prompt return of children wrongfully removed to or retained in any Contracting State" and "to ensure that rights of custody and of access under the law of one Contracting State are effectively respected in the other Contracting States."[240] It distinguishes between "rights of custody" and "rights of access," defining custody rights as including "rights relating to the care of the person of the child and, in particular, the right to determine the child's place of residence."[241] The Convention contains a remedy of return only for "wrongful" removal or retention of a child, which will be found where the removal or retention "is in breach of custody, attributed to a person, an institution or any other body, either jointly or alone, under the law of the State in which the child was habitually resident immediately before the removal or retention" and "at the time of removal or retention those rights were actually exercised, either jointly or alone, or would have been so exercised but for the removal or retention."[242] Since the right of removal is available only for a breach of custodial rights, parents with a right of access and a *ne exeat* clause have argued that the clause gives them a right to determine a child's place of residence and thus a right of custody for purposes of the Convention.

Croll involved a custody order granted by a Hong Kong court in the context of a divorce proceeding between parents of a daughter. The order gave the mother sole custody of the child and the father a right of reasonable access, and included the aforementioned *ne exeat* clause directing that the child not be removed from Hong Kong without the leave of the court or the consent of the other parent. The mother had taken the child to New York City without the knowledge of the father and, while in New York, filed a court action seeking custody, child support, and an order of protection. The father then filed a legal action in the Southern District of New York seeking the child's return to Hong Kong under the Convention.

To determine what constituted "rights of custody" under the Convention, the majority determined the ordinary meaning of the term "custody" from various American dictionary definitions and found that the term implies a primary duty of care and control involving a variety of parental duties. It found that the Convention's use of the plural "rights of custody" implies "a bundle of rights exercised by one or more persons having custody" and considered this concept to be inconsistent with holding a single power such as a veto conferred under a *ne exeat* clause.[243] The court ultimately found that while the clause limited the mother's power to expatriate her daughter, it fell short of conferring a joint right to determine the child's residence. The majority further found that enforcement of rights under a *ne exeat* clause would frustrate the Convention's purposes because it would require delivery of the child to a parent "whose sole right – to visit or veto – imposes no duty to give care."[244] The court cited various sources related to the Convention's drafting as support for its conclusions and further stated that it was not required to defer to "a series of conflicting cases from foreign signatories," finding cases worldwide to be "few, scattered, conflicting, and sometimes conclusory and unreasoned."[245]

In her dissent, Judge Sotomayor argued that the majority had mischaracterized the issue in the case, which she viewed as whether a *ne exeat* clause conferred "rights of custody" under the Convention "wholly independent" of the parent's access rights.[246] In determining the meaning of "rights of custody", she criticized the majority's resort to local definitions of the term "custody" and instead, citing international rules of treaty interpretation to which the United States has long subscribed, looked to the Convention, its object and purposes, and official history, which she found "reflect a notably more expansive concept of custody rights."[247] In her view, the "rights arising under a *ne exeat* clause include the 'right to determine the child's place of residence' because the clause provides a parent with decisionmaking authority regarding a child's international relocation" and thus the clause "vests both Mr. Croll and the Hong Kong court with 'rights of custody' for purposes of the Convention."[248] She found that protecting *ne exeat* rights served the broad purposes of the Convention, which included ensuring that Convention parties respected custody rights under other parties' laws. She further critcized the majority for failing to appreciate the "basic international character" of the Convention, which, she noted, makes the remedy of return available only when cross-border transport of a child takes place and thus protects the broad choice of the country in which a child is to live, as well as the "more specific" choices regarding living arrangements that the majority focused on. Unlike the majority, she also found that the Convention protects custody rights no matter how few a parent possesses. In addition, though stating that it was "not essential" to her conclusion, Judge Sotomayor noted that her analysis was consistent with the decisions of most foreign courts that had considered the issue, examining these cases at some length.[249]

Being a case of first impression, *Croll* set precedent for the Second Circuit regarding an important question under the Hague Child Abduction Convention. Judge Sotomayor approached the Convention with an international perspective, finding it essential to fully explore the Convention to determine the meaning of a term therein and to consider the "basic international character" of the agreement in determining its scope.[250] Finding that the Convention was concerned with cross- border transport, she thus determined that the right to make decisions as to the international relocation of a child inherent in the *ne exeat* clause could be the basis for finding a custody right. She was also attentive to the manner in which the Convention was being implemented in other jurisdictions and to the reasoning of foreign courts ruling on Convention claims, while indicating at the outset that the foreign cases with similar outcomes were complementary to, though not determinative of, her conclusion.

There is currently a split in the circuits as to whether a *ne exeat* clause or right confers a custody right and thus a remedy under the Convention, with the Eleventh Circuit, in *Furnes v. Reeves*, expressly following the *Croll* dissent[251] and the Fourth, Fifth and Ninth Circuits following the *Croll* majority.[252] The issue also remains unsettled internationally, with most case law in the courts of Convention parties reportedly in support of the view that a custody right is so conferred.[253]

While the Supreme Court denied certiorari in both *Croll* and *Furnes*, it currently has an opportunity to revisit the issue in a petition for certiorari in the recent Fifth Circuit case, *Abbott v. Abbott* (08-645). At the invitation of the Court, the Justice Department filed an amicus brief in May 2009, arguing that review should be granted. Finding that *Abbott* was erroneously decided because it failed to give effect to the Convention's broad definition of custody rights, the Department stated that review is merited since the decision "deepens the disagreement among the circuit courts ... and deviates from the majority of courts in States parties that have considered the issue."[254]

Alienage Jurisdiction

Koehler v. Bank of Bermuda[255] involved the scope of alienage jurisdiction under 28 U.S.C. § 1332(a), which grants federal courts diversity jurisdiction in cases between "citizens of a State and citizens or subjects of a foreign state." The Second Circuit had held that alienage jurisdiction was lacking in a case involving a U.S. plaintiff and defendants that were residents or corporations of Bermuda on the ground that Bermuda defendants were not "citizens or subjects of a foreign state." Judge Sotomayor was one of three judges who strongly dissented from the court's subsequent denial of a rehearing *en banc*, arguing that a rehearing "would provide a much-needed opportunity to reexamine the flawed and internationally troublesome position that corporations and individuals from territories of the United Kingdom do not fall within the alienage jurisdiction of the federal courts."[256] The Supreme Court later rejected the majority's approach in its reversal of another Second Circuit ruling.[257]

The Second Circuit had based its ruling in *Koehler* on its 2-1 decision in *Matimak Trading Co. v. Khalily*, which held that Hong Kong, at the time a British Dependent Territory, was not a "foreign state" and thus a corporation established under its law was not a "subject " or "citizen" thereof. [258] Since the United States recognized Bermuda as a British Overseas Territory (the term subsequently used by the United Kingdom for such jurisdictions), and not as a foreign state, the court found that Bermuda had the same status as Hong Kong and that under *Matimak* it was required to hold that diversity jurisdiction was lacking.[259]

Arguing for the rehearing, Judge Sotomayor cited a number of factors intended to show the increasing tenuousness of the majority's approach: the strong negative reaction to the cases by the United Kingdom; the State Department's advocacy of a contrary rule to avoid international controversy for failure to provide a neutral federal judicial forum for the affected foreign persons;

the fact that the Second Circuit was alone in its rulings; the existence of an earlier Second Circuit case that had assumed alienage jurisdiction where a Bermuda corporation was involved; and reservations about *Matimak* expressed in a footnote later added to *Koehler* by two of the judges who ruled in the case.[260] After a detailed analysis of the merits of the issue, Judge Sotomayor concluded that "*Matimak* misapplied the terms 'citizens or subjects of a foreign state' in a fashion inconsistent with both the historical understanding of these terms and a contemporary understanding of the relationship between the United Kingdom and its overseas territories."[261] Finding that constitutional and legislative history called for a broad interpretation of the terms "citizen" and "subject," Judge Sotomayor found that when the State Department "determines that a country is not a sovereign state, the more reasonable conclusion is not that its corporations are 'stateless,' but rather that they are subject to another sovereign."[262] She concluded that Bermuda corporations are subject to the sovereignty of the United Kingdom, a position that she noted is consistent with that of the State Department, the Department of Justice, and the Government of the United Kingdom itself.[263]

Judge Sotomayor concluded by emphasizing that alienage jurisdiction was established by the U.S. Constitution and early statutes to strengthen U.S. relations, particularly commercial ones, with foreign countries and that the importance of these goals had continually increased "as both international relations and global trade have become more complex and our nation has assumed a central role in both."[264] Noting the "clear split" in the circuits and "the potential damage to relations between the United States and the United Kingdom and other nations," she expressed hope that the Supreme Court would choose to address the issue "expeditiously."[265] Two years later, the Supreme Court, overturning a different Second Circuit case, unanimously ruled that individuals and firms of the British Virgin Islands, also a British Overseas Territory, were citizens of the United Kingdom.[266]

Judge Sotomayor vigorously argued that the majority's statutory interpretation was erroneous in light of U.S. law and history. In emphasizing that its interpretation would deny a "considerable number" of foreign entities and individuals – i.e., those nationals and firms of overseas territories of sovereign states that do business with U.S. persons – the "opportunity to adjudicate their claims in a federal forum,"[267] she also indicated an underlying concern that increased international controversy would stem from the majority approach. Because Judge Sotomayor's legal conclusion at the time had considerable support in other circuits as well as increasing support in her own, her concern with the negative international ramifications of the majority's conclusion, along with her attention to governmental positions in the case, seemingly indicates an inclination on her part to remove needless obstacles to fruitful political and commercial relations between the United States and foreign countries.

Common Law Revenue Rule

European Community v. RJR Nabisco[268] involved the application of the common law "revenue rule," under which courts decline to enforce foreign tax judgments or unadjudicated tax claims, to a civil RICO suit brought by the European Communities, its member states, and departments of Colombia against a variety of tobacco companies. An earlier Second Circuit decision, *Attorney General of Canada v. R.J. Reynolds Tobacco Holdings, Inc.* ("*Canada*"), had held that the rule applied to a civil RICO suit filed by the Government of Canada against various Canadian and American tobacco firms.[269] Both cases involved allegations that the defendants had participated in schemes to smuggle contraband cigarettes into the plaintiffs' territories and thereby committed RICO violations – e.g., conspiracies to commit mail and wire fraud – that resulted in the governments' loss of revenue from tobacco duties and taxes and law enforcement costs.

Writing for the court in *European Community*, Judge Sotomayor held that *Canada* was controlling and that in the absence of mitigating factors the revenue rule applied, barring plaintiffs' claims. The Supreme Court later vacated the judgment and remanded the decision for further consideration in light of the Court's ruling in *Pasquantino v. United States*[270] that the revenue rule did not bar a government prosecution of wire fraud under 18 U.S.C. § 1343 connected to a scheme to smuggle liquor into Canada to avoid heavy import taxes. On remand, Judge Sotomayor concluded that *Pasquantino* did not "cast doubt" on the prior Second Circuit ruling – the court standard that would have permitted a different outcome on remand – and reinstated the earlier opinion. As it had in *Canada*, the Supreme Court denied review.

In the court's initial ruling, Judge Sotomayor explained that *Canada* articulated two concerns behind the revenue rule: sovereignty and separation of powers. First, "claims by foreign sovereigns invoking their tax statutes may embroil the courts in an evaluation of the foreign nation's social policies, an inquiry that can be embarrassing to that nation and damaging to the forum state."[271] Second, "because the conduct of foreign relations is primarily the realm of the legislative and executive branches, judicial examination and enforcement of foreign tax laws at the behest of other nations may conflict with the other branches' foreign policy choices with respect to cooperation in tax enforcement and create the risk that the judiciary will be 'drawn into issues and disputes that are assigned to – and better handled – by the political branches of government.'"[272] Where these concerns are not present, however, the rule need not be applied. Under *Canada*, this would occur if the executive branch expressed its consent to the suit or, absent such consent, if the plaintiffs "establish that superior law, such as the federal statute that provides that applicable right of action, abrogates the rule in the context in which the plaintiffs seek to enforce their tax laws."[273] Given that abrogation of the long-standing common law revenue rule in any one case would necessarily have an impact on foreign relations, Judge Sotomayor found that the task required a showing that Congress had directly spoken to the matter. She rejected claims that a subsequent amendment to the RICO statute in the USA PATRIOT Act abrogated the rule – an argument that cited, *inter alia*, the deletion of an amendment that would have codified *Canada* – finding that Congress had not evidenced a clear intent to do so. She also rejected plaintiffs' attempts to show the absence of foreign policy concerns, finding, *inter alia*, that the fact that the Executive Branch was aware of the suit but did not intervene did not constitute consent to the action.

In *Pasquantino*, the Supreme Court had concluded that the case at issue was not intended to recover a foreign tax liability, like a suit to enforce a judgment," but instead "a criminal prosecution brought by the United States in its sovereign capacity to punish domestic criminal conduct."[274] It further found that the sovereignty and separation of powers concerns underlying the revenue rule were obviated when a governmental prosecution is involved, and that the revenue rule thus did not apply to the wire fraud case. In the post-*Pasquantino* reconsideration, Judge Sotomayor stated that these sovereignty and separation of powers were critical because of the exceptions they implied and noted the Supreme Court's finding that government prosecutions overcame the potential problems the rule sought to avoid. She found that since the civil RICO suit was not brought by a foreign government and the executive branch had not expressed its consent to the action, the factors that led the Supreme Court to hold the revenue rule inapplicable to the wire fraud prosecutions in *Pasquantino* were absent in the current case. In citing the lack of U.S. government intervention, the court noted that in both *Canada* and *Pasquantino* the United States had argued that the revenue rule did not bar criminal prosecutions, but did apply to civil cases brought by foreign governments involving direct or indirect attempts to enforce their tax laws. The court dismissed other plaintiff arguments, ultimately stating that since the substance of a claim was the violation of foreign tax laws and since the political branches had not participated in the litigation, there was no reason for *Pasquantino* to disturb the court's earlier conclusion.

As can be seen, Judge Sotomayor was reluctant to involve the judiciary in the resolution of this dispute, paying great attention to the role that the political branches could play in a civil suit of this type and requiring clear evidence that they had before she would allow the litigation to go forward. Finding such evidence lacking, she barred the RICO suit on the basis of earlier Second Circuit precedent. She displayed a desire to adhere to this precedent until the Supreme Court had clearly ruled with respect to the statute at issue in her case. Further, she showed an inclination to defer to the executive branch in a case with foreign policy implications in two ways: first, by respecting executive branch silence and second, by indicating that deference would likely be accorded to its views once expressed. Regarding executive branch views, she noted arguments in earlier executive branch court briefs that such civil RICO cases were not permitted and insisted that any intervention by the executive branch be affirmatively expressed.

LABOR LAW/ANTITRUST[275]

In *Clarett v. National Football League*,[276] the Second Circuit reversed a district court decision that found the NFL's three-year eligibility rule in violation of federal antitrust laws. The three- year rule requires a player to wait at least three full seasons after his high school graduation before entering the NFL draft. Judge Sotomayor, writing for the court, concluded that the three- year rule is protected from antitrust scrutiny by the non-statutory labor exemption to the antitrust laws.[277] Unlike the district court, which evaluated the petitioner's claim in accordance with a test first adopted by the U.S. Court of Appeals for the Eighth Circuit, Judge Sotomayor considered the claim in light of three Second Circuit decisions involving the non-statutory exemption and the concerted activities of a professional sports league.[278]

The Second Circuit maintained that the relationships among sports leagues and their players are governed by collective bargaining agreements, subject to the carefully structured regime established by federal labor laws and not the antitrust laws:

> [T]o permit antitrust suits against sports leagues on the ground that their concerted action imposed a restraint upon the labor market would seriously undermine many of the policies embodied by these labor laws, including the congressional policy favoring collective bargaining, the bargaining parties' freedom of contract, and the widespread use of multi- employer bargaining units.[279]

The Second Circuit viewed the three-year rule as a mandatory subject of collective bargaining and rejected the argument that antitrust law should permit a player to circumvent the bargaining scheme established by federal labor law. The court noted that as a permissible, mandatory subject of bargaining, the conditions "under which a prospective player ... will be considered for employment as an NFL player are for the union representative and the NFL to determine."[280]

ENVIRONMENTAL LAW[281]

Judge Sotomayor 's name is attached to only a small number of environmental decisions, of which she actually wrote in two. The most important of these, partly because it was recently reviewed by the Supreme Court, is *Riverkeeper, Inc. v. US EPA.*[282] *Riverkeeper* addressed an environmental problem caused by the voracious appetite of large power plants for water to cool their facilities. The daily withdrawal from the nation's waterways by such facilities amounts to billions of gallons, destroying in the process a huge number of aquatic organisms. Responding to the problem, Congress, in Clean Water Act (CWA) section 316(b), required that cooling water intake structures reflect the "best technology available" (BTA) for minimizing adverse environmental impact.[283] EPA issued the challenged rule implementing section 316(b) – governing BTA at large, existing power plants ("Phase II" Rule) – in 2004.

The most significant argument against EPA's Phase II Rule addressed by *Riverkeeper* was that EPA had impermissibly construed section 316(b) to allow determination of BTA based on cost- benefit analysis. Judge Sotomayor, writing for the unanimous Second Circuit panel, agreed. First, she noted that CWA sections cross-referenced in section 316(b) demonstrate that after 1989, cost is a lesser, more ancillary consideration in determining what technology EPA must require under those sections. This shift, she wrote, signaled Congress' intent in the CWA to move away from cost-benefit analysis. Second, Judge Sotomayor stated that the language of section 316(b) "plainly indicates that facilities must adopt the *best* technology available" (emphasis by the court), so that cost-benefit analysis cannot be justified.[284]

Judge Sotomayor did not altogether preclude considerations of cost in setting BTA. Rather, she said (drawing on an earlier Second Circuit decision on BTA rules for *new* power plants), costs may be considered to a limited extent, in two ways – to determine what technology can be reasonably borne by the industry, and to evaluate cost-effectiveness. That is, EPA must first determine the most effective technology that may reasonably be borne by the industry in question, then, using that technology as a benchmark, EPA may consider other factors, including cost-effectiveness, to choose a less expensive technology that achieves the same result. Because the administrative record for the rulemaking was unclear as to the basis for the technologies selected by EPA as BTA, and thus may have included the impermissible basis of cost-benefit analysis, the court remanded the Phase II Rule to EPA for clarification and possible reassessment of BTA.

Of the 13 arguments advanced by the parties before the Second Circuit, Supreme Court review was sought on only one – the above cost-benefit issue. On this issue, Judge Sotomayor was reversed 6-3.[285] Writing for the majority, Justice Scalia found that EPA had permissibly relied on cost-benefit analysis in setting BTA and in providing for cost-benefit variances from that standard as part of the Phase II regulations. He deemed it "eminently reasonable to conclude that § 1326(b)'s silence is meant to convey nothing more than a refusal to tie the agency's hands as to whether cost-benefit analysis should be used ...."[286] The significance of this decision stems from the ubiquity of the debate over the role of cost-benefit analysis in environmental statutes. Industry favors such analysis; environmentalists, arguing that environmental factors are often undervalued in cost-benefit analyses, oppose its use. The analysis adopted by the *Entergy* majority may dispose courts to find federal agency authority to use cost-benefit analysis whenever the statute is not explicit one way or the other.

An important climate change case argued before a Second Circuit panel presided over by Judge Sotomayor may also figure in the nomination process. The reason: oral argument occurred three years ago (June 7, 2006), but a decision has yet to be rendered. On the other hand, the Second Circuit is reportedly slow compared to other circuits in rendering opinions, reportedly ranking 11th out of the 13 circuits. The lead clerk of the circuit has been quoted recently as saying that the Second Circuit has seen a "crushing number of immigration filings" over the last decade.[287]

The case involves an attempt to use the common law to reduce the CO2 emissions that contribute to climate change. In 2004, eight states (CA, CT, IA, NJ, NY, RI, VT, WI), New York City, and environmental groups sued five electric utility companies chosen as allegedly the five largest CO_2 emitters in the United States. Invoking the federal and state common law of public nuisance, plaintiffs sought an injunction requiring defendants to abate their CO_2 contribution to the nuisance of climate change. A similar suit filed the same day in the same court added a private nuisance claim. In 2005, the district court dismissed the cases on political question grounds,[288] and the case was argued to the Second Circuit in 2006, as mentioned.

This case involves the conscripting of an ancient common law theory to deal with a modern, complex, and global problem and poses tough questions for the court as to causation and remedy. The Southern District of New York and two other district courts have chosen to avoid the merits of common law claims based on greenhouse gas emissions by calling the matter a political question, unsuitable for resolution by the courts.[289] Nonetheless, the current prominence of the climate change issue in Congress may direct that body's attention to this case.

SECURITIES LAW[290]

Judge Sotomayor has written opinions in several cases involving securities law. Five of these cases are discussed below. Four of the five cases discussed, as do most cases involving federal securities laws, concern allegations of violations of the general antifraud provision of the Securities Exchange Act,[291] referred to as section 10(b), and the rule issued by the Securities and Exchange Commission (SEC) to implement the statute, referred to as Rule 1 0b-5.[292] Because the issues concerning section 10(b) and Rule 1 0b-5 in these four cases were very different, they are discussed separately. The fifth case concerned the fair fund provision of the Sarbanes-Oxley Act.[293] All of the five opinions appear to focus primarily upon the analysis of statutes and cases and display a methodical approach to statutory interpretation. As a group, Judge Sotomayor 's opinions in the securities context appear to favor neither corporations nor investors.

Preemption by the Securities Litigation Uniform Standards Act

SLUSA was enacted in response to the perceived failure of the Private Securities Litigation Reform Act of 1995 (PSLRA)[294] to curb alleged abuses of securities fraud litigation. PSLRA set out a framework for bringing securities fraud cases in federal courts. In many instances, plaintiffs circumvented PSLRA by bringing cases in state courts on the basis of common law fraud or other non-federal claims. By requiring securities fraud cases to be brought only in federal court and only under a uniform standard, SLUSA attempted to make certain that plaintiffs could not avoid the PSLRA requirements. Specifically, SLUSA required suits to be brought in federal rather than state court if: (1) the lawsuit is a covered class action; (2) the claim is based upon state statutory or common law; (3) the claim concerns a covered security; (4) the plaintiff alleges a misrepresentation or omission of a material fact; and (5) the misrepresentation or omission is made *in connection with* the purchase or sale of a covered security.

Dabit v. Merrill Lynch, Pierce, Fenner & Smith, Inc.[295] involved two separate appeals brought by former and current Merrill Lynch brokers (Dabit) and by a Merrill Lynch retail brokerage customer (IJG Investments), which were consolidated by the Second Circuit. In both cases, plaintiffs alleged that Merrill Lynch had issued biased research and investment recommendations in order to obtain investment banking business. The district court had dismissed the plaintiffs' earlier claims as preempted by the Securities Litigation Uniform Standards Act of 1998 (SLUSA).[296] The issue on appeal was whether Congress had intended SLUSA to preempt such actions brought in state courts.

Judge Sotomayor wrote the opinion for the Second Circuit. The court first examined the language of section 10(b) and Rule 1 0b-5. It found that the "in connection with" requirement of SLUSA should be interpreted in the same way that courts have interpreted the phrase in the Securities Exchange Act's general antifraud provision and in the SEC's implementing Rule. In its analysis of past cases which have interpreted this statute and Rule, the court stated that the fraud at issue must be "integral to the purchase and sale of the securities in question."[297] Further, the opinion relied on a Supreme Court case, *Blue Chip Stamps* v. *Manor Drug Stores*,[298] in which the Court had held that a private litigant may bring an antifraud action only if he is an actual purchaser or seller of the securities in question.

Judge Sotomayor 's opinion also considered judicial interpretations of the "in connection with" requirement and the standing of a private litigant in the context of the antifraud provision in order to determine whether standing under SLUSA would be comparable and whether SLUSA could be found to preempt all claims that might be brought under state law. The court found that in enacting SLUSA Congress sought only to ensure that class actions which satisfy the actual purchaser-seller requirement are subject to the federal securities laws. Thus, the court held that, because the *Dabit* plaintiff was a holder and not a buyer or seller of the securities, the suit was not preempted by SLUSA.

In April 2005, four months after the Second Circuit's decision in *Dabit*, the Seventh Circuit adopted an approach opposite to the Second Circuit's. The Seventh Circuit held in *Kircher* v. *Putnam Funds Trust*[299] that "SLUSA is as broad as § 10(b) itself and that limitations on private rights of action to enforce § 10(b) and Rule 1 0b-5 do not open the door to litigation about securities transactions under state law."[300] The Seventh Circuit opinion states that "it would be more than a little strange if the Supreme Court's decision to block private litigation by non- traders became the opening by which that very litigation could be pursued under state law, despite the judgment of Congress (reflected in SLUSA) that securities class actions must proceed under federal securities law or not at all."[301]

In September 2005, the United States Supreme Court granted the petition for writ of certiorari to the United States Court of Appeals for the Second Circuit, presumably to resolve the split between the Second and Seventh circuit approaches.[302] The Supreme Court unanimously[303] vacated the judgment of the Second Circuit, rejecting the Second Circuit's holding (i.e., that the operative language of "in connection with" must be read narrowly to preempt only those actions in which the purchaser-seller requirement of *Blue Chip Stamps* is met).[304]

To support its holding, the Court discussed the legislative history, concluding that Congress must have been aware of the broad construction of the phrase "in connection with the purchase or sale" adopted by both the Court and the Securities and Exchange Commission when Congress used this key phrase in SLUSA:

> And when "judicial interpretations have settled the meaning of an existing statutory provision, repetition of the same language in a new statute indicates, as a general matter, the intent to incorporate its ... judicial interpretations as well."[305]

To buttress its holding that Congress intended a broad interpretation of "in connection with the purchase or sale," the Court stated:

> The presumption that Congress envisioned a broad construction follows not only from ordinary principles of statutory construction but also from the particular concerns that culminated in SLUSA's enactment. A narrow reading of the statute would undercut the effectiveness of the 1995 Reform Act and thus run contrary to SLUSA's stated purpose, viz., "to prevent certain State private securities class action lawsuits alleging fraud from being used to frustrate the objectives of the 1995 Act.[306]

Finally, in response to the argument that the holder class action brought by respondent was distinguishable from a typical class action because it was not brought by a required purchaser or seller of the securities, the Court stated that the identity of the plaintiffs does not determine whether the compliant alleges fraud "in connection with the purchase or sale" of securities:

> The misconduct of which respondent complains here—fraudulent manipulation of stock prices—unquestionably qualifies as fraud "in connection with the purchase or sale" of securities as the phrase is defined....[307]

Deference to SEC

In *Press v. Quick & Reilly, Inc.*,[308] plaintiffs, who are former and current clients of the defendant broker-dealers, brought suit because the broker-dealers allegedly made automatic sweeps of the clients' uninvested funds into money market funds which were poor performers. Plaintiffs alleged violations of section 10(b) Rule 1 0b-5, and Rule 1 0b- 10.[309]

Writing for the court, Judge Sotomayor discussed the SEC's finding that the general disclosures made by the fund prospectuses were sufficient and stated that it is bound by the SEC's interpretations of its regulations unless they are "plainly erroneous or inconsistent.... "[310] In the instant case, according to the court, the interpretation was not clearly erroneous or inconsistent. The Second Circuit went on to find that any omissions which may have occurred were not material.

Insider Trading: Misappropriation Theory

In *United States v. Falcone*,[311] Joseph Falcone appealed from a conviction of several counts of securities fraud. A stockbroker acquaintance of the defendant's had received pre-release copies of a column in *Business Week* magazine from an employee of Hudson News, a magazine wholesaler. The stockbroker used the information to trade securities and passed on the information to the defendant, who also traded securities based upon the confidential information. The conviction of the defendant by the lower court turned upon the misappropriation theory of insider trading. According to this theory, a person violates section 10(b) and Rule 10b-5 "when he misappropriates material nonpublic information in breach of a fiduciary duty or similar relationship of trust and confidence and uses that information in a securities transaction. In contrast to [the traditional theory], the misappropriation theory does not require that the buyer or seller of securities be defrauded."[312] The defendant claimed that the United States Supreme Court's decision in *United States v. O 'Hagan*[313] vitiated the lower court's decision that his securities trading satisfied the "in connection with" the purchase or sale of a security requirement of section 10(b). The Second Circuit, in an opinion by Judge Sotomayor, affirmed the lower court's conviction.

The Second Circuit held that Falcone misappropriated material nonpublic information as the misappropriation theory requirements were laid out in *O'Hagan*. According to the court, the Supreme Court's not laying out all of the parameters of the misappropriation of inside information did not absolve Falcone from his actions. After *O'Hagan*, for example, the Second Circuit had applied the misappropriation theory to schemes involving nontrading tippers and had not discussed the "in connection with" requirement.[314] In *Falcone*, according to the Second Circuit, the government had to prove only that the tipper owed a duty to the owner of the misappropriated information and that the defendant/tippee knew that the tipper had breached his duty.[315] The court found that sufficient evidence was introduced at trial from which a reasonable jury could deduce that the government had proved its case.

Standing

In *In re NYSE Specialists*,[316] lead plaintiff investors appealed from the lower court's judgment granting the New York Stock Exchange's (NYSE) motion to dismiss claims that it had failed to regulate fairly and their claim under Rule 1 0b-5 that the NYSE had made misrepresentations about the integrity of the market. Lead plaintiffs argued that the lower court erred in its finding that the NYSE is entitled to absolute immunity and in its finding that the plaintiffs lacked standing under Rule 10b-5 to bring suit against the NYSE for misrepresentations about its integrity and internal operations.

In an opinion by Judge Sotomayor, the Second Circuit affirmed the lower court's judgment as to the NYSE's absolute immunity for its alleged regulatory failures but vacated the ruling that plaintiffs lacked standing under Rule 10b-5. As for the NYSE's absolute immunity, the court stated that the Securities and Exchange Commission has "formidable oversight power to supervise, investigate, and discipline the NYSE for any possible wrongdoing or regulatory missteps."[317] However, the court vacated the lower court's decision concerning plaintiffs' lack of standing to sue under Rule 10b-5, stating that the lower court's determination that a plaintiff's cause of action under Rule 10b-5 for false statements about a purchased security lies only against the issuer of the security was incorrect.

Sarbanes-Oxley

In *Official Committee of Unsecured Creditors of World-Com, Inc. v. Securities and Exchange Commission*,[318] various unsecured creditors of WorldCom appealed a lower court order approving a plan by the SEC for the distribution of money to victims of the WorldCom securities fraud. The distribution of the funds was based upon the fair funds provision of the Sarbanes-

Oxley Act,[319] which permits the amount of any civil penalty for disgorgement obtained by the SEC against a person violating the securities laws to be added to the fund for the benefit of the victims of the violation. The Committee argued that the distribution plan wrongfully excluded certain categories of creditors and that the lower court did not apply the correct standard of review.

The Second Circuit affirmed the lower court decision. Writing for the court, Judge Sotomayor held that, because the lower court had only to determine that the SEC's distribution plan "fairly and reasonably distributed the limited Fair Fund proceeds among the potential claimants,"[320] she was satisfied that the lower court had not abused its discretion in its findings.

TAXATION[321]

Judge Sotomayor has not written extensively in the area of taxation, and it is not possible to draw conclusions about her judicial philosophy from the tax cases in which she has been involved. One the Supreme Court, while agreeing with the holding, expressly disagreed with her reasoning. In that case, *William L. Rudkin Testamentary Trust v. Comm'r,*[322] the issue was whether investment- advice fees incurred by a trust were "costs which are paid or incurred in connection with the administration of the ... trust and which would not have been incurred if the property were not held in such trust ...."[323] If so, the fees were fully deductible; if not, they were only partially deductible as miscellaneous itemized deductions. At the time the Second Circuit heard the case, a split had developed among the other circuits. The Sixth Circuit had held the fees were fully deductible,[324] while the Fourth and Federal Circuits reached the opposite conclusion after finding the provision only applied to expenses that were not customarily incurred by individuals.[325]

Writing for the court, Judge Sotomayor agreed with the holding of the Fourth and Federal Circuits, but used a different analysis. Looking at the statute's plain meaning, she found it only applied to those expenses that *could* be incurred by an individual. This was an objective inquiry and did not require a subjective determination of whether an individual *would* have incurred such expenses. The court disagreed with the interpretation by the Fourth and Federal Circuits because it found "nothing in the statute [to] indicate[] that Congress intended the [provision] to give rise to factual disputes about whether an individual asset owner is insufficiently financially savvy or the assets sufficiently large such that he or she unquestionably would have sought investment advice."[326]

The Supreme Court, in a unanimous decision written by Chief Justice Roberts, affirmed the Second Circuit's holding, but rejected its reasoning.[327] According to the Court, an analysis focusing on whether such fees *could* have been incurred by an individual "flies in the face of the statutory language" since "the fact that an individual could not do something is one reason he would not, but not the only possible reason."[328] Congress would have used "could" had it wanted and "[t]he fact that it did not adopt this readily available and apparent alternative strongly supports rejecting the Court of Appeals' reading."[329] The Court also concluded that the Second Circuit's interpretation made part of the statute superfluous. Instead, the Court adopted the analysis of the other circuits, finding the common meaning of the term "would" required a determination as to whether the fees would customarily be incurred if the property was held by an individual. Finding that it was not uncommon for an individual to seek investment advice, the Court held the fees were not fully deductible.

Thus, while both the Second Circuit and Supreme Court held the fees were partially deductible, the Court expressly disavowed Judge Sotomayor 's reasoning and adopted an interpretation that she had explicitly rejected. The case is interesting because both the Second Circuit and Supreme Court performed a straight-forward statutory interpretation analysis, looking only at the plain language of the statute,[330] yet came to different conclusions about what the term "would" meant in the context of the statute. Judge Sotomayor, in writing for the Second Circuit, developed an interpretation—one apparently not pursued by either party before the court or adopted by the other appellate courts—that seemed intended to avoid complexity in the tax statute. The government, in fact, subsequently adopted her analysis before the Supreme Court, characterizing it as the preferred interpretation "because it makes the statute significantly easier to administer."[331] On the other hand, while her intent was perhaps laudatory, it could be criticized, and was by the Supreme Court, for being inconsistent with the common meanings of the terms in the statute.

GOVERNMENT CONTRACTORS AND *BIVENS* ACTIONS[332]

Judge Sotomayor wrote the opinion in *Malesko v. Correctional Services Corporation*,[333] a Second Circuit decision that would have allowed "Bivens actions" against government contractors but was reversed 5-4 by the Supreme Court.[334] Bivens actions take their name from a 1971 case in which the Supreme Court recognized a cause of action for damages against federal officials for violations of individuals' Fourth Amendments rights.[335] Later courts expanded *Bivens* to allow claims against federal officials for failure to provide due process under the Fifth Amendment and cruel and unusual punishment in violation of the Eighth Amendment.[336] The plaintiff in *Malesko* alleged that his Eighth Amendment rights were violated by a contractor of the Federal Bureau of Prisons, whose employee required him to climb the stairs despite a known heart condition. While climbing the stairs, he suffered a heart attack, fell, and was injured.

Key to the Second Circuit's decision was its finding that the Supreme Court's decision in *FDIC v. Meyer*, which held that individuals may not bring Bivens actions against federal agencies, was not dispositive because "private entities acting on behalf of the federal government are not the equivalent of federal agencies."[337] The opinion specifically noted differences between federal agencies and government contractors regarding the deterrent effects and fiscal implications of *Bivens* actions.[338] It further noted the improbability of the Supreme Court implicitly overruling numerous pre-*Meyer* cases allowing *Bivens* claims against government contractors and the similarities between *Bivens* actions and actions under 42 U.S.C. § 1983, which allows suits against contractors of state governments for constitutional violations.[339]

Judge Sotomayor 's opinion might suggest that her approach to the purpose and expansion of *Bivens* actions differs from that of the majority in the 2001 Supreme Court *Malesko* case. Judge Sotomayor 's *Malesko* opinion characterizes providing a remedy for constitutional violations as a "more important goal of *Bivens* liability" than deterring wrongdoing by individuals.[340] The Supreme Court, in contrast, emphasized the deterrence goals of *Bivens*.[341] In addition, her opinion in *Malesko* would have expanded *Bivens* by allowing plaintiffs to bring actions for damages against government contractors based on their employees' violations of plaintiffs' constitutional rights. In contrast, the Supreme Court "refused to extend *Bivens* liability to any new context or new category of defendants."[342]

The Supreme Court has not extended *Bivens* since 1980, and some commentators have read its decisions as signaling a desire to abolish *Bivens* actions.[343] However, such a characterization might overstate the significance of *Malesko* and, particularly, one sentence in it, given that four other Circuits allowed Bivens actions against contractors prior to *Malesko*[344] and the *Malesko* opinion largely focuses on issues other than the relative importance of the "goals" of *Bivens* liability.

Author Contact Information

Anna C. Henning, Coordinator
Legislative Attorney
ahenning@crs.loc.gov, 7-4067

Kenneth R. Thomas,
Coordinator Legislative Attorney
kthomas@crs.loc.gov, 7-5006

Cynthia Brougher
Legislative Attorney
cbrougher@crs.loc.gov, 7-9121
Vivian S. Chu
Legislative Attorney
vchu@crs.loc.gov, 7-4576

Jody Feder
Legislative Attorney
jfeder@crs.loc.gov, 7-8088

Michael John Garcia
Legislative Attorney
mgarcia@crs.loc.gov, 7-3873

Jeanne J. Grimmett
Legislative Attorney
jgrimmett@crs.loc.gov, 7-5046

Nancy Lee Jones
Legislative Attorney
njones@crs.loc.gov, 7-6976

Erika K. Lunder
Legislative Attorney
elunder@crs.loc.gov, 7-4538

Kate M. Manuel
Legislative Attorney
kmanuel@crs.loc.gov, 7-4477

Robert Meltz
Legislative Attorney
rmeltz@crs.loc.gov, 7-7891

Kathleen Ann Ruane
Legislative Attorney
kruane@crs.loc.gov, 7-9135

Michael V. Seitzinger
Legislative Attorney
mseitzinger@crs.loc.gov, 7-7895

Jon O. Shimabukuro
Legislative Attorney
jshimabukuro@crs.loc.gov, 7-7990

Alison M. Smith
Legislative Attorney
amsmith@crs.loc.gov, 7-6054

Gina Stevens
Legislative Attorney
gstevens@crs.loc.gov, 7-2581

Carol J. Toland
Legislative Attorney
ctoland@crs.loc.gov, 7-4659

L. Paige Whitaker
Legislative Attorney
lwhitaker@crs.loc.gov, 7-5477

End Notes

[1] In what is perhaps the best-known case in connection with Justice Souter, *Planned Parenthood v. Casey*, 505 U.S. 833, 854 (1992), he joined a plurality opinion which upheld *Roe v. Wade*. The plurality opinion stated that "the rule of law underlying our own Constitution requires such continuity over time that a respect for precedent is, by definition, indispensable."

[2] Kelsey v. County of Schoharie, 2009 U.S. App. LEXIS 10985 (2d Cir. 2009).

[3] This portion of the report was prepared by Kathleen Ann Ruane, Legislative Attorney.

[4] U.S. Const. Amdt. I.

[5] *See, e.g.*, Papineau v. Parmley, 465 F.3d 46 (2006). Judge Sotomayor ruled against officers who were arguing for qualified immunity in a civil suit filed against them for violating plaintiff's First Amendment right to protest. When attempting to break up the protest, the officers involved did not order the protestors to disperse. The officers, instead, stood in a line, waited 35 seconds, then charged into the crowd arresting people indiscriminately. Because the circumstances did not appear to suggest imminent harm from the protest, Judge Sotomayor held that the officers should have issued a dispersal order before beginning to arrest people.

[6] 304 F.3d 183 (2d Cir. 2002).

[7] 402 F.3d 304 (2d Cir. 2005). The district court had forbidden the press from publishing the names of the jury in Quattrone's trial, but the judge had made no findings of fact regarding the harms that might flow from such publication and the names of the jurors had been announced, more than once, in open court.

[8] 427 U.S. 539 (1976).

[9] 549 F.3d 861 (2d Cir. 2008).

[10] 380 U.S. 51 (1965).

[11] 549 F.3d at 870-873.

[12] 380 U.S. at 58-59.

[13] 290 F.3d 143 (2d Cir. 2002).

[14] *Id.* at 146 (citing Pickering v. Board of Education, 391 U.S. 563, 568 (1968)).

[15] *Id.* at 154 (Sotomayor, J., dissenting).

[16] *Id.*

[17] *See* Heil v. Santoro, 147 F.3d 103, 109 (2d Cir. 1998).

[18] 524 F.3d 361 (2d Cir. 2008).

[19] *Id.* at 372 (quoting Connick v. Myers, 461 U.S. 138 (1983)).

[20] 297 F.3d 108 (2d Cir. 2002).

[21] *See* Hazelwood Sch. Dist. v. Kuhlmeier, 484 U.S. 260 (1988); Bethel School Dist. No. 403 v. Fraser, 478 U.S. 675 (1986); Tinker v. Des Moine Indep. Cmty. Sch. Dist., 393 U.S. 503 (1969).

[22] 461 F.3d 320 (2d Cir. 2006). Judge Sotomayor voted to uphold a student's right to wear a T-shirt which depicted President George W. Bush in an unflattering light. (The shirt implied that the President had abused drugs.) The panel found that the T-shirt was not offensive or inappropriate; therefore, according to the Supreme Court, the student may only be prevented from wearing it if doing so caused substantial disruption to school functioning. The parties agreed that the shirt had not caused substantial disruption to school function and therefore could not constitutionally be censored.

[23] 527 F.3d 41 (2d Cir. 2008) (student disqualified for student government position after posting a statement on a blog about a school event). The panel noted that the Supreme Court had not ruled definitively upon the scope of school authority over off-campus speech, but applied Second Circuit precedent which held that students can be disciplined for expressive conduct occurring outside of school if it would "foreseeably create a risk of substantial disruption in the school environment." Because the speech at issue in the case related to a school event, contained vulgar language and clear inaccuracies, and precipitated many e-mails and phone calls to school officials, the court found the speech rose to the level at which it might be permissibly punished by school officials.

24 This portion of the report was prepared by Cynthia Brougher, Legislative Attorney.

25 *See, e.g.,* Salazar v. Buono, 527 F.3d 758 (9th Cir. 2008), *cert. granted*, 129 S.Ct. 1313 (2008) (No. 08-472); Petition for a Writ of Certiorari, Navajo Nation v. U.S. Forest Service, No. 08-846 (U.S. filed Jan. 5, 2009).

26 441 F.3d 96 (2d Cir. 2006).

27 *Id.*

28 *Id.* at 109 (Sotomayor, J., dissenting).

29 *Id.* at 118. The Second Circuit had not adopted the ministerial exception, but each of the eight circuit courts to consider the ministerial exception has recognized it to some extent. Although there appears to be consensus regarding the ministerial exception, the extent to which religious organizations may make employment decisions for non-clergy positions remains controversial.

30 *See* Application of the Religious Freedom Restoration Act to the Award of a Grant Pursuant to the Juvenile Justice and Delinquency Prevention Act, Memorandum Opinion for the General Counsel Office of Justice Programs, U.S. Department of Justice (June 29, 2007), http://www.usdoj.gov/olc/2007/worldvision.pdf.

31 *See* Joint Statement of Senator Hatch and Senator Kennedy, 146 Cong. Rec. 16,698, 16,699 (July 27, 2000) (inserted in general debate as Exhibit 1) ("Whether from indifference, ignorance, bigotry, or lack of resources, some institutions restrict religious liberty in egregious and unnecessary ways.").

32 Ford v. McGinnis, 352 F.3d 582 (2d Cir. 2003) (holding that prison officials were not entitled to summary judgment because they had not shown "that legitimate penological interests justified their conduct" in denying a prisoner a religious holiday meal significant to his religious practice); Salahuddin v. Mead, 174 F.3d 271 (2d Cir. 1999) (holding that a prisoner's First Amendment claim could proceed because the prisoner filed the action prior to the enactment of the Prison Litigation Reform Act, which required administrative remedies be exhausted before a lawsuit could be brought. Thus, the exhaustion requirement did not apply to the prisoner's claim).

33 *Ford*, 352 F.3d at 589-90 (internal quotations omitted).

34 *See* Navajo Nation v. U.S. Forest Service, 535 F.3d 1058 (9th Cir. 2008), *cert. petition filed*, No. 08-846 (U.S. Jan. 5, 2009).

35 *Ford*, 352 F.3d at 593.

36 *Id.* ("To confine the protection of the First Amendment to only those religious practices that are mandatory would necessarily lead us down the unnavigable road of attempting to resolve intra-faith disputes over religious law and doctrine.").

37 *Id.* at 593-94.

38 This portion of the report was prepared by Vivian S. Chu, Legislative Attorney.

39 128 S. Ct. 2783 (2008). For more on the Supreme Court's decision, see CRS Report R40137, *District of Columbia v. Heller: The Supreme Court and the Second Amendment*, by Vivian S. Chu.

40 Specifically, the three provisions ruled unconstitutional were: (1) D.C. Code § 7-2502.02, which generally barred the registration of handguns; (2) D.C. Code § 22-4504, which prohibited carrying a pistol without a license, insofar as the provision would prevent a registrant from moving a gun from one room to another within his home; and (3) D.C. Code § 7-2507.02, which required that all lawfully owned firearms be kept unloaded and disassembled or bound by a trigger lock or similar device. 128 S. Ct. at 2817-19.

41 92 U.S. 542, 553 (1875).

42 116 U.S. 252 (1886).

43 128 S. Ct. at 2813, n.23.

44 *Id.* (citing Presser v. Illinois, 116 U.S. 252, 265 (1886); Miller v. Texas, 153 U.S. 535, 538 (1894)).

45 554 F.3d 56 (2d Cir. 2009) (petition for *writ of certiorari* pending).

46 A "chuka stick" (or "nunchuka") is defined as "any device designed primarily as a weapon, consisting of two or more lengths of a rigid material joined together by a thong, rope or chain ...

capable of being rotated in such a manner as to inflict serious injury upon a person." *Id.* at 58 (citing N.Y. Penal Law § 265.01(1)).

[47] *Maloney*, 554 F.3d at 58.

[48] *Id.* at 59 (quoting Rodriguez de Quijas v. Shearson/Am. Express, Inc., 490 U.S. 477, 484 (1989)).

[49] Nordyke v. King, 563 F.3d 439 (9th Cir. 2009).

[50] *Id.* at 450.

[51] *Id.* at 457. The Ninth Circuit, however, went on to hold that the county ordinance prohibiting possession of firearms on county property did not violate the Second Amendment because it fits within the exception for "sensitive places" that *Heller* recognized. *Id.* at 460.

[52] Nat'l Rifle Ass'n v. City of Chicago, Illinois and Village of Oak Park, Illinois, Nos. 08-4241, 08-4245 & 08-4244, slip op. at 3 (7th Cir. Jun 2, 2009) (affirming the lower courts' decisions to dismiss suits against cities on the ground that *Heller* dealt with law enacted under the authority of the national government, while Chicago and Oak Park are subordinate bodies of a state).

[53] *Id.* at 4.

[54] This portion of the report was prepared by Kenneth R. Thomas, Legislative Attorney.

[55] 442 F.3d 30 (2d Cir. 2004).

[56] U.S. Const., Art. 8, cl.3. provides that "The Congress shall have Power ... To regulate Commerce with foreign Nations, and among the several States, and with the Indian Tribes."

[57] 514 U.S. 549 (1995).

[58] 18 U.S.C. § 922(q)(1)A).

[59] U.S. v. Corp, 236 F.3d 325 (6th Cir. 2001) (overturning conviction of twenty-three males convicted of possessing pornographic pictures of 17-year old girls made from materials shipped in interstate commerce, relationship to child pornography industry attenuated); United States v. McCoy , 323 F.3d 1114 (9th Cir. 2003) (overturning criminal conviction based on one picture, made from materials shipped in interstate commerce, of a mother and her child with exposed genitals, as attenuated from commercial activity). *But see* United States v. Gallenardo, 540 F. Supp. 2d 1172 (9th Cir. 2007) (suggesting that the Supreme Court overruled the reasoning of *McCoy* in Gonzales v. Raich, 545 U.S. 1 (2005)).

[60] United States v. Morrison, 529 U.S. 598, 610-12 (four factors to be considered in determining the existence of a "substantial effect" on commerce include whether (1) the activity at which the statute is directed is commercial or economic in nature; (2) the statute contains an express jurisdictional element involving interstate activity that might limit its reach; (3) Congress has made specific findings regarding the effects of the prohibited activity on interstate commerce; and (4) the link between the prohibited conduct and a substantial effect on interstate commerce is not attenuated.

[61] For instance, the Court in *Lopez* held that the power to regulate and protect the instrumentalities of interstate commerce existed "even though the threat may only come from intrastate activities." *Lopez*, 514 U.S. at 558.

[62] 545 U.S. at 21. U.S. Const., Art. 1, § 8, cl. 18 provides that "[The Congress shall have Power].... To make all Laws which shall be necessary and proper for carrying into Execution the foregoing Powers, and all other Powers vested by this Constitution in the Government of the United States, or in any Department or Officer thereof."
Clause 18: Necessary And Proper Clause.

[63] The opinion did note in a footnote that " ... our conclusion is consistent with that of the majority of other Circuits that have considered this question. *See* Holston, 343 F.3d at 88 n.2 (collecting cases)." *Harris*, 358 F.3d at 223 n. 2.

[64] 343 F.3d 83 (2d Cir. 2003).

[65] "The fact that Harris challenges a provision located in a different section of the Act is a distinction without a difference. There is simply no basis for drawing a constitutional distinction between the two sections." *Harris*, 358 F.3d at 223.

[66] This portion of the report was prepared by Michael John Garcia, Legislative Attorney.

[67] *See* Boumediene v. Bush, 128 S.Ct. 2229 (2008) (ruling 5-4 that the constitutional writ of *habeas corpus* extends to non-citizens held at the U.S. Naval Station in Guantanamo Bay, Cuba);

Hamdan v. Rumsfeld, 548 U.S. 557 (2006) (ruling 5-3 that military tribunals established by the President did not comply with the Uniform Code of Military Justice or the law of war which the Code incorporated, including the 1949 Geneva Conventions). In the case of Hamdi v. Rumsfeld, 542 U.S. 507 (2004), concerning the authority of the President to detain a U.S. citizen as an enemy combatant, no opinion was joined by a majority of the justices. However, in separate opinions, five justices recognized the President's authority, acting pursuant to the 2001 Authorization to Use Military Force (P.L. 170-40), to detain enemy belligerents captured on the battlefield in Afghanistan. *Hamdi*, 542 U.S. at 518 (four-justice plurality opinion of O'Connor, J.); *id.* at 588-589 (Thomas, J., dissenting).

[68] *See* discussion in the section on "Fourth Amendment," *infra.*

[69] 471 F.3d 67 (2d Cir. 2006).

[70] *See* discussion in the section on "First Amendment: Free Speech," *supra.*

[71] John Doe, Inc. v. Mukasey, 549 F.3d 861 (2d Cir. 2008).

[72] Arar v. Ashcroft, 414 F.Supp.2d 250 (E.D.N.Y. 2006).

[73] Arar v. Ashcroft, 532 F.3d 157 (2d Cir. 2008). Judge Sotomayor was not on the circuit panel.

[74] A video of the oral arguments is available at [http://www.c-spanarchives.org/library/index.php?mainjage=product_video_info&products_id=282779-1]. Perhaps because of the limited number of national security cases adjudicated by Judge Sotomayor, some observers have examined her questioning during oral arguments in Arar v. Ashcroft for clues as to her views on national security matters. Attention has been drawn to Judge Sotomayor's questioning of the government's attorney during oral arguments; in particular, her question, "So the minute the Executive raises the specter of foreign policy, it is the government's position that that is a license to torture?". Some have suggested that Judge Sotomayor's questioning evidences skepticism regarding broad claims of executive authority on national security matters. *See* Gene Healy, Op-Ed, Sotomayor: *A Presidential Power Skeptic?*, *Washington Examiner*, June 9, 2009. However, a line of questioning during oral arguments is not always indicative of a judge's legal conclusions or eventual ruling in a case.

[75] This portion of the report was prepared by Jody Feder, Legislative Attorney.

[76] 530 F. 3d 87 (2d Cir. 2008).

[77] Ricci v. DeStefano, 129 S. Ct. 894 (2009).

[78] 42 U.S.C. § 2000e-2.

[79] U.S. Const. amend. XIV, § 1.

[80] Ricci v. DeStefano, 554 F. Supp. 2d 142, 160 (D. Conn. 2006).

[81] *Id.* at 161-62.

[82] Ricci v. Destefano, 530 F.3d at 87 (2d Cir. 2008).

[83] Robert Barnes and Eli Saslow, *Bias Case Looms Large for Nominee; Ruling on Firefighters' Lawsuit Raises Questions About Sotomayor's Philosophy*, Washington Post, May 31, 2009 at A01.

[84] 243 F.3d 610 (2d Cir. 2001).

[85] *Id.* at 628.

[86] 202 F.3d 560 (2d Cir. 2000).

[87] *Id.* at 567.

[88] *Id.* at 571.

[89] *Id.* at 572.

[90] 195 F.3d 134 (2d Cir. 1999) (Sotomayor, J., dissenting).

[91] For more information on 42 U.S.C. §§ 1981 and 1983, see CRS Report RL33386, *Federal Civil Rights Statutes: A Primer*, by Jody Feder.

[92] 195 F.3d at 151-53.

[93] 368 F.3d 123 (2d Cir. 2004).

[94] *Id.* at 124-25.

[95] 196 F.3d 89 (2d Cir. 1999). The court also addressed the plaintiff's disability discrimination claims; these claims are discussed elsewhere in this report. *See* discussion in section on "Civil Rights: Individuals with Disabilities," *infra.*

[96] 373 F.3d 310 (2d Cir. 2004). The officers also alleged malicious prosecution and retaliation in violation of the First Amendment.
[97] *See* discussion in the section on "Religious Freedom Restoration Act," *supra.*
[98] 441 F.3d 96 (2d Cir. 2006) (Sotomayor, J., dissenting).
[99] *Id.* at 109.
[100] *Id.* at 109-15.
[101] *Id.* at 118.
[102] This portion of the report was prepared by Nancy Lee Jones and Carol J. Toland, Legislative Attorneys.
[103] For a more detailed discussion of Judge Sotomayor's decisions in this area see CRS Report R40640, *Civil Rights of Individuals with Disabilities: The Opinions of Judge Sotomayor*, by Nancy Lee Jones and Carol J. Toland.
[104] 42 U.S.C. § 12101 *et seq.* For a more detailed discussion of the ADA, see CRS Report 98-92 1, *The Americans with Disabilities Act (ADA): Statutory Language and Recent Issues*, by Nancy Lee Jones.
[105] 29 U.S.C. § 794. *See* Pell v. Columbia University, 1998 U.S. Dist. LEXIS 407 (S.D.N.Y. Jan 21, 1998).
[106] For a more detailed discussion of Section 504 of the Rehabilitation Act, see CRS Report RL34041, *Section 504 of the Rehabilitation Act of 1973: Prohibiting Discrimination Against Individuals with Disabilities in Programs or Activities Receiving Federal Assistance*, by Nancy Lee Jones.
[107] 42 U.S.C. § 10801 *et seq.*
[108] 42 U.S.C. § 10801(b).
[109] 20 U.S.C. § 1400 *et seq.*
[110] For a detailed discussion of IDEA as amended by the 2004 reauthorization, see CRS Report RL32913, *The Individuals with Disabilities Education Act (IDEA): Interactions with Selected Provisions of the No Child Left Behind Act (NCLB)*, by Richard N. Apling and Nancy Lee Jones, and CRS Report R40521, *The Individuals with Disabilities Education Act (IDEA): Supreme Court and Selected Lower Court Decisions*, by Nancy Lee Jones and Carol J. Toland.
[111] *See, e.g.,* Valentine v. Standard & Poor's, 50 F.Supp.2d 262 (S.D.N.Y. 1999), where Judge Sotomayor rejected an ADA employment discrimination claim stating: "the ADA does not immunize disabled employees from discipline or discharge for incidents of misconduct in the workplace." *Id.* at 289.
[112] 2001 U.S. District LEXIS 11926 (S.D.N.Y. Aug. 15, 2001). *See, e.g.*, Jim Dwyer, *On the Bench with Fairness and Empathy*, New York Times A-21 (May 27, 2009). This decision was the final one in a long procedural odyssey. 970 F. Supp. 1094 (S.D.N.Y. 1997) (opinion by Judge Sotomayor), *reconsideration denied*, 2 F. Supp. 2d 388 (S.D.N.Y. 1997) (opinion by Judge Sotomayor), *aff'd in part, vacated in part*, 156 F.3d 321 (2d Cir. 1998), *vacated remanded by* 527 U.S. 1031 (1999), *aff'd in part, vacated in part, remanded in part*, 226 F.3d 69 (2d Cir. 2000), *on remand*, 2001 U.S. District LEXIS 11926 (S.D.N.Y. Aug. 15, 2001) (opinion by Judge Sotomayor).
[113] P.L. 110-325. For a more detailed discussion see CRS Report RL34691, *The ADA Amendments Act: P.L. 110-325*, by Nancy Lee Jones.
[114] A colloquy was held during the House debates on the ADA Amendments Act between Representatives Pete Stark and George Miller on the subject of the meaning of "substantially limits" in the context of learning, reading, writing, thinking, or speaking. The colloquy found that an individual who has performed well academically may still be considered an individual with a disability. 153 Cong. Rec. H. 8291 (September 17, 2008).
[115] 464 F.3d 229 (2d Cir. 2006).
[116] 1998 U.S. Dist. LEXIS 407 (S.D.N.Y. Jan. 21, 1998).
[117] *Compare* Lloret v. Lockwood Greene Engineers, Inc., 1998 U.S. Dist. LEXIS 3999 (S.D.N.Y. 1998) *and* Brown v. Parkchester South Condominiums, 287 F.3d 58 (2d Cir. 2002).

[118] *See, e.g.*, Protection & Advocacy for Persons with Disabilities v. Mental Health & Addiction Services, 448 F.3d 119 (2d Cir. 2006).

[119] *See, e.g.*, Bartlett v. New York State Board of Bar Examiners, 1998 U.S. Dist. LEXIS 407 (S.D.N.Y. Jan. 21, 1998); Norville v. Staten Island University,196 F.3d 89 (2d Cir. 1999); Taylor v. Vermont Department of Education *et al.*, 313 F.3d 768 (2d Cir. 2002).

[120] Parker v. Columbia Pictures Industries, 204 F.3d 326 (2d Cir. 2000); Protection & Advocacy for Persons Disabilities v. Mental Health & Addiction Services, 448 F.3d 119 (2d Cir. 2006).

[121] Erik W. Robelen, *School Rulings by Sotomayor Eyed,* Education Week, June 5, 2009, http://www.edweek.org/ew/ articles/2009/06/10/33sotomayor-2.h28.html?tkn=PXZFVopNh%2BllvMFiMtnJ1 S6WDo5b9VocboEX&print=1 (quoting Perry A. Zirkel, Professor of Education and Law at Lehigh University).

[122] This portion of the report was prepared by L. Paige Whitaker, Legislative Attorney.

[123] 470 F.3d 458 (2d Cir. 2006).

[124] The candidate, Verena Rivera-Powell, also argued that the Board of Elections denied her equal protection of the laws by removing her name from the ballot because of her race. This claim was found to be was found to be without merit because the allegation of racial discrimination was conclusory. See *id.* at 470.

[125] *See id.* at 466-67 (citing Cleveland Bd. of Educ. v. Loudermill, 470 U.S. 532, 545-46 (1985)).

[126] *Id.* at 467.

[127] *Id.* at 468.

[128] *Id.* at 469.

[129] *Id.* (citing Shannon v. Jacobowitz, 394 F.3d 90, 96 (2d Cir. 2005)).

[130] 449 F.3d 305 (2d Cir. 2006).

[131] *See* 42 U.S.C. § 1973.

[132] *Hayden*, 449 F.3d at 310.

[133] *Id.* at 313 (citing Baker v. Pataki, 85 F.3d 919 (2d Cir. 1996) (*en banc*)).

[134] *Id.* (citing Johnson v. Gov. of State of Florida, 405 F.3d 1214 (11th Cir. 2005) (*en banc*), Farrakhan v. Washington, 359 F.3d 1116 (9th Cir. 2004)).

[135] 519 U.S. 337, 341 (1997) (stating "the plainness or ambiguity of statutory language is dictated by the language itself, the specific context in which that language is used, and the broader context of the statute as a whole").

[136] *Hayden*, 449 F.3d at 367 (Sotomayor, J., dissenting).

[137] *Id.* at 367-68.

[138] *Id.* at 368.

[139] *Id.*

[140] This portion of the report was prepared by Jon O. Shimabukuro, Legislative Attorney.

[141] *See supra* note 6 and accompanying text.

[142] 304 F.3d 183 (2d Cir. 2002

[143] The restriction on federal funds to foreign nongovernmental organizations is referred to as the "Mexico City Policy" because it was first announced at a 1984 United Nations conference in Mexico City. Pursuant to the Mexico City Policy, foreign nongovernmental organizations that were interested in receiving U.S. government funds had to agree to a provision called the "standard clause" in family planning agreements and contracts with the United States Agency for International Development. The standard clause prohibited the organizations from engaging in activities that promoted abortion. In January 2009, President Barack Obama rescinded the Mexico City Policy. For additional information on the Mexico City Policy, see CRS Report RL3 3250, *International Population Assistance and Family Planning Programs: Issues for Congress*, by Luisa Blanchfield.

[144] 915 F.2d 59 (2d Cir. 1990).

[145] *CRLP*, 304 F.3d at 190.

[146] 494 F.3d 296 (2d Cir. 2007), *cert. denied*, 128 S.Ct. 2472 (2008).

[147] *Id.* at 309.

[148] *Id.* at 327.

[149] *Id.* at 330-3 1.
[150] 497 F.3d 201 (2d Cir. 2007).
[151] *Id.* at 202.
[152] *Id.*
[153] *Id.* at 203-04. Although the BIA acknowledged that a number of circuit courts of appeals had suggested that nonviolent, involuntary IUD insertions might constitute persecution, it nevertheless concluded in *Zheng* that involuntary insertion did not constitute persecution.
[154] *Id.* at 203 ("The BIA's opinion in Zheng's case was non-precedential and was signed by a single member of the Board.").
[155] This portion of the report was prepared by Gina Stevens, Legislative Attorney.
[156] Tigue v. Department of Justice, 312 F.2d 70 (2d Cir. 2002); Wood v. Federal Bureau of Investigation, 432 F.3d 78 (2d Cir. 2005). Judge Sotomayor joined a few other opinions in FOIA cases that resulted in issuance of summary orders by the Second Circuit. She also authored an opinion addressing the Privacy Act of 1974. *See* Bechhoefer v. Department of Justice, 209 F.3d 57 (2d Cir. 2000) (holding that "record" under the Privacy Act has a "broad meaning encompassing" any personal information "about an individual that is linked to that individual through an identifying particular").
[157] 5 U.S.C. § 552.
[158] 5 U.S.C. § 552(b).
[159] 5 U.S.C. § 552(b)(5).
[160] See, e.g., Michael N. Kennedy, Comment, Escaping the Fishbowl: A Proposal To Fortify The Deliberative Process Privilege, 99 Nw. U.L. Rev. 1769, 1789 (2005); Michael Ray Harris, Standing In The Way of Judicial Review: Assertion of the Deliberative Process Privilege in APA Cases, 53 St. Louis L. J. 349 (2009).
[161] 312 F.3d 70 (2d Cir. 2002), *cert. denied*, Tigue v. DOJ, 538 U.S. 1056 (2003).
[162] 532 U.S. 1 (2001) .
[163] *Tigue*, 312 F.3d at 80 (citing Grand Cent. P'ship v. Cuomo, 166 F.3d 473 (2d Cir. 1989)).
[164] 421 U.S. 132 (1975).
[165] *Tigue*, 312 F.3d at 74 -74. The memo is referenced in a footnote, and an excerpt of the memo is quoted in the Commission's Report.
[166] *Id.* at 81 (citing Access Reports v. Dep't of Justice, 926 F.2d 1192 (D.C. Cir. 1991); Common Cause v. IRS, 646 F.2d 656, 660 (D.C. Cir. 1981)).
[167] Wood v. Federal Bureau of Investigation, 432 F. 3d 78 (2d Cir. 2005).
[168] 5 U.S.C. § 552(b)(6).
[169] 456 U.S. 595 (1982).
[170] *Id.* at 599, 602.
[171] *Id.* at 600.
[172] 432 F. 3d 78 (2d Cir. 2005).
[173] *Id.* at 86 (citing Dep't of State v. Washington Post Co., 456 U.S. 595, 601 (1982)).
[174] *Id.* (citing Dep't of State v. Ray, 502 U.S. 164, 175 (1991)).
[175] *Id.* (citing *Washington Post Co.*, 456 U.S. at 600-01).
[176] This portion of the report was prepared by Anna C. Henning and Alison M. Smith, Legislative Attorneys.
[177] *See, e.g.*, Jess Bravin and Nathan Koppel, *Nominee's Criminal Rulings Tilt to Right of Souter*, Wall St. J. June 5, 2009 at A3.
[178] U.S. Const. amend. IV.
[179] *See* Kyllo v. United States, 533 U.S. 27, 34 (2001); United States v. Place, 462 U.S. 696, 716 (1983) (Brennan, J., concurring in result).
[180] *See* Atwater v. City of Lago Vista, 532 U.S. 318, 354 (2001).
[181] 230 F.3d 44 (2d Cir. 2000).
[182] 382 F.3d 225 (2d Cir. 2004).
[183] 445 U.S. 573 (1980).
[184] *Id.* at 589-90.

[185] 427 U.S. 38 (1976).
[186] *Id.* at 65.
[187] 382 F.3d 225 (2d Cir. 2004) (Sotomayor, J., concurring in part and dissenting in part).
[188] Griffin v. Wisconsin, 483 U.S. 868, 873 (1986) (citing New Jersey v. T.L.O., 469 U.S. 325, 351 (1985) (Blackmun, J., concurring)).
[189] *N.G. ex rel. S.C*, 382 F.3d at 239 (Sotomayor, J., dissenting).
[190] 266 F.3d 64 (2d Cir. 2001).
[191] *Id.* at 73 (citing Nat'l Treasury Employees Union v. Von Raab, 489 U.S. 656, 65 (1989)).
[192] 480 U.S. 709 (1987).
[193] *Id.* at 75 (citing *O'Connor*, 480 U.S. at 726).
[194] 471 F.3d 67 (2d Cir. 2006).
[195] *See supra* note 69 and accompanying text.
[196] Maritime Transportation Security Act of 2002, 46 U.S.C. §§ 70101-70119.
[197] 489 F.3d 484 (2d Cir. 2007).
[198] Although it was not termed the "exclusionary rule" until later, the Supreme Court first clearly articulated a remedy of excluding evidence as a result of Fourth Amendment violations in *Weeks v. United States*. 232 U.S. 383, 393 (1914) ("If letters and private documents can thus be seized and held and used in evidence against a citizen accused of an offense, the protection of the Fourth Amendment ... is of no value"). Although the Weeks holding applied only to evidence obtained by federal officers, the Court later applied the rule to the states in *Mapp v. Ohio*. 367 U.S. 643, 655 (1961).
[199] 468 U.S. 897, 922 (1984).
[200] 514 U.S. 1 (1995).
[201] See *id.*
[202] In an opinion in another case, *United States v. Estrada*, 430 F.3d 606 (2d Cir. 2005), Judge Sotomayor also found an exception to the exclusionary rule in the Fifth Amendment context. As in *Santa* and *Falso* in the Fourth Amendment context, she applied a Supreme Court precedent with facts similar to those in *Estrada*, holding that because the defendant had stated that he had a gun in his pocket, the "public safety" exception to the Fifth Amendment exclusionary rule, which typically applies to exclude evidence collected as a result of questioning that was not preceded by *Miranda* warnings, was applicable.
[203] 544 F.3d 110 (2d Cir. 2008).
[204] 426 F.3d 68 (2d Cir. 2005).
[205] 180 F.3d 20, 24 (2d Cir. 1999).
[206] *Id.* at 24.
[207] 129 S. Ct. 1692 (2009).
[208] *Santa*, 180 F.3d at 26; *Herring*, Slip op. at 1 (Breyer, J., dissenting) (both quoting Evans, 514 U.S. at 15).
[209] Under § 1983, state and local employees may be held civilly liable for depriving a person of "any rights, privileges, or immunities secured by the Constitution and laws."
[210] Harlow v. Fitzgerald, 457 U.S. 800, 818 (1982).
[211] 175 F.3d 99 (2d Cir. 1999).
[212] *Id.* at 105 (citing Cartier v. Lussier, 955 F.2d 841, 845 (2d Cir. 1992)).
[213] *Id.* at 106.
[214] 339 F.3d 129 (2d Cir. 2003).
[215] *Id.* at 137 (quoting Glass v. Mayas, 984 F.2d 55, 58 (2d Cir. 1993)).
[216] 517 F.3d 140 (2d Cir. 2008).
[217] 460 U.S. 325 (1983).
[218] 496 F.3d 139 (2d Cir. 2007).
[219] *Id.* at 144.
[220] *Id.* at 167.
[221] *Id.* at 169.

[222] 465 F.3d 46 (2d Cir. 2006). In addition to the Fourth Amendment issues discussed here, plaintiffs in *Papineau* also claimed damages for violations of their First Amendment rights. *See supra* note 5 and accompanying text.

[223] *Id.* at 53.

[224] 490 U.S. 386 (1989

[225] 28 U.S.C. § 2254(d).

[226] 28 U.S.C. § 2254(d)(1); *See also,* Williams v. Taylor, 529 U.S. 362, 405-406 (2000) (stating that a state court's decision is "contrary to" clearly established law if it "applies a rule that contradicts the governing law set forth in our cases" or if it "confronts a set of facts that are materially distinguishable from a decision of this Court and nevertheless arrives at a result different from our precedent").

[227] It is worth noting that no capital case from Vermont, Connecticut or New York has reached the Second Circuit during normal review. Thus, Judge Sotomayor's opinions have involved non-capital *habeas* cases.

[228] 252 F.3d 630 (2001).

[229] 476 U.S. 79 (1986) (holding that prosecutors may not use race as a factor in peremptory challenges).

[230] The dissent argued that the defendant's failure to object rendered the claim meritless under *Batson.*

[231] *Galarza*, 252 F.3d at 638.

[232] 260 F.3d 87 (2001).

[233] *Id.* at 97 (referring to Illinois v. Allen, 397 U.S. 337 (1970) (holding that a defendant can lose his Sixth Amendment right to be present at his own trial if, after a trial judge's warning that he will be removed if he continues his disruptive behavior, he continues to be disorderly and disruptive); Taylor v. United States, 414 U.S. 17 (1973) (rejecting petitioner's claim that his voluntary absence from his trial constitutes a wavier without a demonstration that that the trial court expressly warned him that the trial would continue in his absence)).

[234] 442 F.3d 770. (2006).

[235] Anders v. California, 386 U.S. 738 (1967) (establishing process by which an attorney can conclude that the appeal is frivolous and ask to withdraw from the case or have the court dispose of the case without the filing of merits briefs). *Anders* also requires an attorney to refer "to anything in the records that might arguably support the appeal." *Id.* at 744.

[236] 528 U.S. 470 (2000) (stating that if an attorney unreasonably fails to file a notice of appeal, this failure also gives rise to a presumption of prejudice).

[237] *Camp usano*, 442 F.3d at 774.

[238] This section was prepared by Jeanne J. Grimmett, Legislative Attorney.

[239] 229 F.3d 133, 143 (2d Cir. 2000), *cert. denied,* 534 U.S. 949 (2001).

[240] Hague Convention on the Civil Aspects of International Child Abduction art. 1, Oct. 25, 1980, at http://www.hcch.net/index _en.php?act=conventions.pdf&cid=24. The United States became a party to the Convention in 1988. The Convention was implemented in the International Child Abduction Remedies Act, P.L. 100-300, 42 U.S.C. § 11601 *et seq.*

[241] *Id.* art. 5.

[242] *Id.* art. 3.

[243] *Croll*, 229 F.3d at 139.

[244] *Id.* at 140.

[245] *Id.* at 143.

[246] *Id.* at 145 (Sotomayor, J., dissenting).

[247] *Id.* at 145-46.

[248] *Id.* at 146.

[249] *Id.* at 150-53.

[250] *Id.* at 147.

[251] Furnes v. Reeves, 362 F.3d 702, 719 (1 1th Cir. 2004), *cert. denied*, 543 U.S. 978 (2004).

[252] Abbott v. Abbott, 542 F.3d 1081, 1087 (5th Cir. 2008), *petition for cert. filed*, 77 U.S.L.W. 3308 (U.S. Nov. 14, 2008) (No. 08-645); Fawcett v. McRoberts, 326 F.3d 491, 500 (4th Cir. 2003), *cert. denied*, 540 U.S. 1068 (2004); Gonzales v. Gutierrez, 311 F.3d 942, 954 (9th Cir. 2002).

[253] Hague Conference on Private International Law, *Transfrontier Contact Concerning Children: General Principles and a Guide to Good Practice* 43 (2008), at http://hcch.e-vision

[254] Brief for the United States as Amicus Curiae, Abbott v. Abbott, 542 F.3d 1081 (2008)(No. 08-645, at http://www.usdoj.gov/osg/briefs/2008/2pet/6invit/2008-0645.pet.ami.inv.pdf.

[255] 209 F.2d 130 (2d Cir. 2000) (*Koehler I*).

[256] Koehler v. Bank of Bermuda (*Koehler II*), 229 F.2d 187 (2d Cir. 2000).

[257] JP Morgan Bank v. Traffic Stream (BVI) Infrastructure Limited, 536 U.S. 88 (2002).

[258] Matimak Trading Co. v. Khalily, 118 F.3d 76 (2d Cir. 1997), *cert. denied*, 522 U.S. 1091 (1998).

[259] *Koehler I*, 209 F.3d at 139.

[260] *Id.* at 189. For the text of the subsequently added note, *see* 229 F.3d 424 (2d Cir. 2000).

[261] Id. at 190-93.

[262] *Id.* at 193.

[263] *Id.* at 193.

[264] *Id.*

[265] *Id.* at 193-94.

[266] *Traffic Stream*, 536 U.S. at 100.

[267] *Id.* at 193.

[268] 355 F.3d 123, 132 (2d Cir. 2004), *judgment vacated and remanded*, 544 U.S. 1012 (2005).

[269] Attorney General of Canada v. R.J. Reynolds Tobacco Holdings, Inc., 268 F.3d 103 (2d Cir. 2001), *cert denied*, 537 U.S. 1000 (2002).

[270] Pasquantino v. United States, 544 U.S. 349, 125 S.Ct. 1766 (2005).

[271] *European Community*, 355 F.3d at 131.

[272] *Id.* at 132 (quoting *Canada*, 268 F.3d at 123).

[273] *European Community*, 355 F.3d at 132.

[274] *Pasquantino*, 125 U.S. at 362, 125 S.Ct. at 1776).

[275] This portion of the report was prepared by Jon O. Shimabukuro, Legislative Attorney.

[276] 369 F.3d 124 (2d Cir. 2004).

[277] The non-statutory exemption to the antitrust laws has been inferred from federal labor statutes to protect the collective bargaining process, even when a collective bargaining agreement results in certain restraints on competition. In contrast, the statutory exemption to the antitrust laws is derived from the texts of the Clayton Act and the Norris- LaGuardia Act, and insulates from antitrust scrutiny certain unilateral conduct of labor groups, such as boycotts and pickets.

[278] *See Clarett*, 369 F.3d at 133 ("We, however, have never regarded the Eighth Circuit's test in *Mackey* as defining the appropriate limits of the non-statutory exemption.").

[279] *Id.* at 135.

[280] *Id.* at 141.

[281] This portion of the report was prepared by Robert Meltz, Legislative Attorney.

[282] 475 F.3d 83 (2d Cir. 2007).

[283] 33 U.S.C. § 1326(b).

[284] *Riverkeeper*, 475 F.3d at 98.

[285] Entergy Corp. v. Riverkeeper, Inc., 129 S. Ct. 1498 (2009).

[286] *Id.* at 1508.

[287] Darren Samuelsohn, *"Mystery" Climate Case Might Become Issue in Sotomayor Confirmation*, Greenwire, June 1, 2009, http://www.eenews.net/Greenwire/2009/06/0 1/archive/1?terms=sotomayor

[288] Connecticut v. American Electric Power, 406 F. Supp. 2d 265 (S.D.N.Y. 2005).

[289] California v. GMC, 2007 U.S. Dist. LEXIS 68547 (N.D.Cal. 2007); Colo. ex rel. Suthers v. Gonzales, 558 F. Supp. 2d 1158 (Dist.Colo. 2007); Conn. v. Am. Elec. Power Co., 406 F.Supp.2d 265 (S.D.N.Y. 2005).

[290] This portion of the report was prepared by Michael V. Seitzinger, Legislative Attorney.

[291] 15 U.S.C. § 78j(b).
[292] 17 C.F.R. § 240.10b-5.
[293] 15 U.S.C. § 7246(a).
[294] P.L. 104-67, 109 Stat. 737.
[295] 395 F.3d 25 (2d Cir. 2005).
[296] 15 U.S.C. §§ 77p, 78bb(f).
[297] *Dabit*, 395 F.3d at 37.
[298] 421 U.S. 723 (1975).
[299] 403 F.3d 478 (7th Cir. 2005).
[300] *Id.* at 484.
[301] *Id.*
[302] No. 04-1371.
[303] Justice Alito took no part in the consideration of the case.
[304] Merrill Lynch, Pierce, Fenner & Smith v. Dabit, 547 U.S. 71 (2006).
[305] *Id.* at 85.
[306] *Id.* at 86.
[307] *Id.* at 89.
[308] 218 F.3d 121 (2d Cir. 2000).
[309] 17 C.F.R. § 10b-10 requires a broker-dealer to disclose to its customers any remuneration which it receives from third parties in connection with a customer transaction.
[310] *Press*, 218 F.3d at 128 (quoting Auer v. Robbins, 519 U.S. 452, 461-63 (1997)).
[311] 257 F.3d 226 (2d Cir. 2001).
[312] United States v. Chestman, 947 F.2d 551, 566 (2d Cir. 1991).
[313] 521 U.S. 642 (1997). In very general terms, *O'Hagan* held that a person may be held liable for violating section 10(b) and Rule 10b-5 if he misappropriates nonpublic information which he has obtained from having a fiduciary relationship with a reporting company and then trades the securities of that company for personal gain.
[314] *See, e.g.*, United States v. Mc Dermott, 245 F.3d 133 (2d Cir. 2001).
[315] United States v. Libera, 989 F.2d 596, 600 (2d Cir. 1993).
[316] 503 F.3d 89 (2d Cir. 2007).
[317] *Id.* at 101.
[318] 467 F.3d 73 (2d Cir. 2006).
[319] 15 U.S.C. § 7246(a).
[320] *Official Committee*, 467 F.3d at 85.
[321] This portion of the report was prepared by Erika K. Lunder, Legislative Attorney.
[322] 467 F.3d 149 (2d Cir. 2006).
[323] 26 U.S.C. § 67(e).
[324] O'Neill v. Comm'r, 994 F.2d 302 (6th Cir. 1993).
[325] Mellon Bank, N.A. v. United States, 265 F.3d 1275 (Fed. Cir. 2001); Scott v. United States, 328 F.3d 132 (4th Cir. 2003).
[326] *Rudkin*, 467 F.3d at 155.
[327] Knight v. Comm'r, 128 S. Ct. 782 (2008).
[328] *Id.*
[329] *Id.*
[330] As Judge Sotomayor explained in *Rudkin*, when interpreting a statute, courts "'start ... with the language of the statute,'" giving the terms "'their ordinary, contemporary, common meaning, absent an indication Congress intended them to bear some different import.'" Rudkin, 467 F.3d at 15 1-52 (quoting Williams v. Taylor, 529 U.S. 420, 431 (2000)). "'[The court's] inquiry must cease if the statutory interpretation is unambiguous and the statutory scheme is coherent and consistent.'" *Id.* at 152 (quoting Robinson v. Shell Oil Co., 519 U.S. 337, 340 (1997)). Otherwise, the court may look at the statute's legislative history for guidance. *See id.* Here, neither court examined the provision's legislative history.
[331] Brief of Appellee-Respondent at 17, Knight v. Comm'r, 128 S. Ct. 782 (2008) (No. 06-1286).

[332] This portion of the report was prepared by Kate M. Manuel, Legislative Attorney.

[333] Malesko v. Correctional Servs. Corp., 229 F.3d 374 (2000), *rev 'd*, Correctional Servs. Corp. v. Malesko, 534 U.S. 61 (2001).

[334] In the Supreme Court's decision, Chief Justice Rehnquist wrote the majority opinion, in which Justices O'Connor, Scalia, Kennedy, and Thomas joined. Justice Stevens filed a dissenting opinion in which Justices Souter, Ginsburg, and Breyer joined. Several of the Justices in the majority are no longer on the court, but their replacements might not depart from their views on this issue.

[335] See Bivens v. Six Unknown Named Agents of the Fed. Bureau of Narcotics, 403 U.S. 388, 397 (1971).

[336] *See* Carlson v. Green, 446 U.S. 14 (1980) (Eighth Amendment); Davis. v. Passman, 442 U.S. 228 (1979) (Fifth Amendment).

[337] *Malesko*, 229 F.3d at 380 (discussing FDIC v. Meyer, 510 U.S. 471 (1994)).

[338] The opinion suggested that suits against contractors have a greater effect in deterring individual wrongdoing than suits against federal agencies because "employer[s] facing exposure to such liability would be motivated to prevent unlawful acts by ... employees." It also suggested that even if contractors passed on the costs of *Bivens* liability to federal agencies, their doing so would not have the same direct effect on federal fiscal policy that subjecting federal agencies to Bivens claims would have.

[339] *Id.* at 381 (discussing Lugar v. Edmondson Oil Co., 457 U.S. 922, 936-37 (1982), which allowed a claim under Section 1983 against a contractor of a state agency).

[340] *Id.* at 380 ("Although deterring wrongdoing by individuals is an important goal of *Bivens* liability, we find an extension of such liability to be warranted even absent a substantial deterrent effect in order to accomplish the more important *Bivens* goal of providing a remedy for constitutional violations").

[341] *Malesko,* 534 U.S. at 70 ("The purpose of *Bivens* is to deter individual[s] ... from committing constitutional violations.").

[342] *Id.* at 68.

[343] *See, e.g.*, Jeffrey M. Nye, Holly v. Scott: *Constitutional Liability of Private Correctional Employees and the Future of Bivens Jurisprudence*, 75 U. Cin. L. Rev. 1245, 1248 (2007).

[344] 229 F.3d at 381.

In: Judge Sonia Sotomayor: Selected Options
Editors: Patrick K. Reed
ISBN: 978-1-60876-759-5

Chapter 3

The Nomination of Judge Sonia Sotomayor: A Review of Second Circuit Decisions Relating to Reproductive Rights

Jon O. Shimabukuro

Summary

On May 26, 2009, Judge Sonia Sotomayor of the U.S. Court of Appeals for the Second Circuit was nominated to replace retiring U.S. Supreme Court Justice David H. Souter. During her tenure with the Second Circuit, Judge Sotomayor has not addressed substantive legal questions involving abortion, such as the extent of the Constitution's protection of a woman's right to choose. Judge Sotomayor has, however, authored opinions that have considered the impact of foreign funding restrictions on domestic nonprofit organizations that promote abortion, discussed the effect of forced abortions and involuntary family planning practices in the context of applications for asylum, and examined possible municipal liability resulting from anti-abortion demonstrations. This report reviews Judge Sotomayor's opinions involving abortion and family planning practices.

On May 26, 2009, Judge Sonia Sotomayor of the U.S. Court of Appeals for the Second Circuit was nominated to replace retiring U.S. Supreme Court Justice David H. Souter.[1] During her tenure with the Second Circuit, Judge Sotomayor has not addressed substantive legal questions involving abortion, such as the extent of the Constitution's protection of a woman's right to choose. Judge Sotomayor has, however, authored opinions that have considered the impact of foreign funding restrictions on domestic nonprofit organizations that promote abortion, discussed the effect of forced abortions and involuntary family planning practices in the context of applications for asylum, and examined possible municipal liability resulting from anti-abortion demonstrations.

This report reviews Judge Sotomayor's opinions involving abortion and family planning practices. Some have questioned Judge Sotomayor's position on abortion, particularly in light of her affiliation with the Puerto Rican Legal Defense and Education Fund, which joined other advocacy organizations in promoting abortion rights in amicus briefs filed with the Court between 1980 and 1992. A review of Judge Sotomayor 's opinions on abortion and family planning, however, suggests a respect for precedent and an adherence to established legal standards.[2]

Mexico City Policy

In *Center for Reproductive Law and Policy v. Bush*, the Second Circuit considered an appeal brought by a nonprofit organization devoted to the promotion of reproductive rights.[3] The Center for Reproductive Law and Policy (CRLP) challenged the federal government's policy of conditioning the availability of U.S. government funds for foreign nongovernmental organizations on their agreement to neither perform nor promote abortion. The CRLP argued that the so-called "Mexico City Policy" deprived the organization of its rights to freedom of speech and association under the First Amendment by limiting its interactions and communications with foreign nongovernmental organizations.[4] The CRLP maintained that the Mexico City Policy discouraged foreign nongovernmental organizations from collaborating with it because the organizations feared being viewed as promoting abortion.

The Second Circuit affirmed the district court's dismissal of the CRLP's claim on the grounds that the Mexico City Policy did not prohibit the organization from exercising its First Amendment rights. Writing for the court, Judge Sotomayor relied heavily on *Planned Parenthood Federation of America, Inc. v. Agency for International Development*, a 2002 decision by the Second Circuit that also involved a First Amendment challenge to the Mexico City Policy by a domestic nonprofit organization.[5] Judge Sotomayor explained, "*Planned Parenthood* not only controls this case conceptually; it presented the same issue.

Planned Parenthood rejected the same First Amendment challenge to the same provision ... and no intervening Supreme Court case law alters its precedential value."[6]

While the district court dismissed the CRLP's claim on the grounds that the organization lacked standing under Article III of the Constitution, the Second Circuit reached its decision after considering the merits of the claim and declining to resolve the standing question. After reviewing several decisions by the Supreme Court involving the assumption of standing by a court in order to proceed directly to the merits of a case, the Second Circuit reasoned that where a governmental provision is challenged as unconstitutional and another case has already entertained and rejected the same constitutional challenge to the same provision, a court may dispose of the case on the merits without addressing a novel question of jurisdiction.[7]

Citing *Planned Parenthood*, the Second Circuit maintained that the Mexico City Policy did not implicate any constitutional rights.[8] Domestic nonprofit organizations remained free to use their own funds to pursue abortion-related activities in foreign countries. The decision not to collaborate with the CRLP because of the acceptance of U.S. government funds by a foreign nongovernmental organization had only an "incidental effect" on the activities of the CRLP that did not rise to the level of a constitutional violation.

Involuntary Family Planning Practices and Applications for Asylum

In *Shi Liang Lin v. U.S. Dept. of Justice*, the Second Circuit reviewed three orders issued by the Board of Immigration Appeals (BIA) that denied applications for asylum submitted by three unmarried partners of individuals who were forced to have abortions in China.[9] The BIA's denials were based on its conclusion that spouses of individuals who were forced to abort a pregnancy or submit to involuntary sterilization, but not the unmarried partners of such individuals, could automatically qualify for asylum as refugees under federal immigration law. In reviewing the BIA's orders, the Second Circuit sought to determine whether Section 601(a) of the Illegal Immigration Reform and Immigrant Responsibility Act of 1996, which amended the definition for the term "refugee" to include individuals who were forced to abort a pregnancy or submit to involuntary sterilization, was ambiguous, so that the BIA's construction of the term was entitled to deference.

The Second Circuit evaluated the BIA's interpretation of Section 601(a) in accordance with the principles articulated by the Supreme Court in *Chevron U.S.A. v. NRDC.*[10] In *Chevron*, the Court administers is entitled to deference. First, a reviewing court will consider whether Congress has spoken on the question at issue. If the intent of Congress is clear, the court must "give effect to the unambiguously expressed intent of Congress."[11] If the statute is silent or ambiguous, however, a court will examine whether the agency's interpretation constitutes a permissible construction of the statute.

The Second Circuit rejected the BIA's interpretation of Section 601(a), finding that Congress has spoken unambiguously about who may be deemed a refugee for purposes of asylum eligibility. The court maintained that nothing in the definition for the term "refugee" permits a person to obtain asylum if he or she has not personally experienced persecution or a well-rounded fear of future persecution. The Second Circuit explained,

> We do not deny that an individual whose spouse undergoes, or is threatened with, a forced abortion or involuntary sterilization may suffer a profound emotional loss as a partner and a potential parent. But such a loss does not change the requirement that we must follow the "ordinary meaning" of the language chosen by Congress, according to which an individual does not automatically qualify for "refugee" status on account of a coercive procedure performed on someone else.[12]

Thus, the Second Circuit maintained that Section 601(a) seemed to deny asylum protection to the spouses of individuals forced to abort a pregnancy or submit to involuntary sterilization, as well as the unmarried partners of such individuals.

In a concurring opinion, Judge Sotomayor criticized the majority opinion for its lack of judicial restraint. In response to the majority's conclusion that even spouses of individuals forced to abort a pregnancy or submit to involuntary sterilization may not be automatically eligible for asylum, Judge Sotomayor noted,

> Instead of answering the limited question before us—whether the BIA's denial of asylum to the unmarried partners of women forced to undergo abortions or sterilization was unreasonable—the majority has chosen to go beyond it to address an issue that is unbriefed, unargued, and unnecessary to resolve this appeal.[13]

Judge Sotomayor noted that because Congress did not indicate how direct the harm or injury must be before it can be determined that an individual suffers persecution and should be considered a "refugee" for purposes of asylum protection, the BIA's construction of the term should be entitled to deference so long as it is reasonable. Judge Sotomayor maintained that the majority opinion failed to explain why the harm of forced abortion or sterilization constituted persecution only for the person undergoing the procedure and not for the spouse. Forced abortion, Judge Sotomayor observed, could be devastating for the spouse, as well as the woman:

> The termination of a wanted pregnancy under a coercive population control program can only be devastating to any couple, akin, no doubt, to the killing of a child ... In the end, I fail to understand how the majority can claim that the harm caused by a spouse's forced abortion or sterilization is not a personal harm to both spouses—either or both of whom can be sterilized for violations of the population control programs—especially given the unique biological nature of pregnancy and special reverence every civilization has accorded to child- rearing and parenthood in marriage.[14]

In *Zheng v. Gonzales*, the Second Circuit reviewed a BIA order that dismissed an appeal by a woman seeking asylum based on the involuntary insertion of an intrauterine device (IUD).[15] The immigration judge that first considered the petitioner's case denied her application for asylum on the grounds that IUD implantation did not constitute persecution and that "Congress did not intend to include birth control methods other than abortion or forced sterilization in its definition of persecution ..."[16] The BIA agreed with the immigration judge and noted that Zheng had not been persecuted, in part, because she did not experience a "significant degree of pain or restriction as a result of the procedure."[17] The BIA also acknowledged the widespread use of IUDs as a method of birth control and observed that there is nothing so inherently egregious about the procedure to conclude that Zheng was persecuted.[18]

Judge Sotomayor, writing for the court, remanded the case to the BIA "so that it might articulate its position concerning whether and under what conditions the forced insertion of an IUD constitutes persecution."[19] The BIA had taken contrary positions on whether the involuntary insertion of an IUD constituted persecution, finding in at least one other case that such insertion was persecution.[20] Judge Sotomayor also noted that the BIA had not discussed the issue in a published, precedential opinion.[21] Thus, the BIA's failure to explain when the involuntary insertion of an IUD would constitute persecution "depriv[ed] the bench, the bar and potential asylum applicants of guidance concerning whether and how they might approach the issue."[22]

Municipal Liability and Anti-Abortion Demonstrations

In *Amnesty America v. Town of West Hartford*, five anti-abortion demonstrators and a self-described "pro-life" organization appealed a Connecticut district court decision that granted summary judgment in favor of the Town of West Hartford (Town).[23] The case arose out of two anti-abortion demonstrations at a clinic where abortions were performed. The plaintiffs argued that the Town police used excessive force when they attempted to remove the demonstrators from the premises. Although many demonstrators reportedly suffered pain and physical injuries as a result of their treatment by the police, the district court found that the plaintiffs failed to show that the actions of the police were taken pursuant to a municipal custom or policy. Thus, the district court concluded that the plaintiffs had not established a basis upon which the Town could be held liable for the actions of its police officers.

On appeal, the plaintiffs maintained that the district court erred in granting summary judgment in favor of the Town. They asserted that their proffered evidence raised material issues of fact under two independent theories of municipal liability. First, the plaintiffs claimed that the Town failed to supervise its police force at both demonstrations. They contended that the Town police chief was present at the demonstrations, witnessed the use of excessive force, and failed to stop it. Second, the plaintiffs alleged that the Town acted with deliberate indifference in failing to train its police officers to arrest protesters without using excessive force, even after the Town received complaints about the use of force during the first demonstration.

Writing for the Second Circuit, Judge Sotomayor found that the plaintiffs proffered ample evidence to raise genuine issues of material fact with regard to the Town's failure to supervise its police force.[24] The court maintained, however, that the plaintiffs did not submit sufficient evidence from which a reasonable jury could conclude that the Town was liable for any failure to train its officers.

Citing prior municipal liability decisions by the Supreme Court, as well as the Second Circuit, the court explained that in order to support a failure to supervise claim, the evidence "must establish only that a policymaking official had notice of a potentially serious problem of unconstitutional conduct, such that the need for corrective action or supervision was 'obvious,' (citation omitted) ... and the policymaker's failure to investigate or rectify the situation evidences deliberate indifference, rather than mere negligence or bureaucratic inaction."[25] Applying this standard, the Second Circuit found that the plaintiffs' proffered evidence was sufficient to withstand summary judgment because it allowed the inference that the Town's police chief witnessed the misconduct, and that the actions of the police were so blatantly unconstitutional that his inaction could be the result of deliberate indifference.[26]

However, the Second Circuit concluded that the plaintiffs' evidence failed to raise an inference that the police were improperly trained. Citing Supreme Court precedent, the court noted that municipal liability for failing to train employees requires that a plaintiff establish not only deliberate indifference on the part of officials, but also a specific deficiency in a city's training program and a causal relationship between the deficiency and the misconduct.[27] In this case, the plaintiffs failed to offer any evidence as to the purported inadequacies in the Town's training program and the causal relationship between those inadequacies and the misconduct. The court observed that the use of excessive force could have resulted from other causes, such as the negligent administration of a valid program.[28]

In *Amnesty America*, as well as *Center for Reproductive Law and Policy*, the parties that may arguably be viewed as supporting a "pro-life" position prevailed. At least some of the claims advanced by Amnesty America and the anti-abortion demonstrators were remanded, and the dismissal of the CRLP's case was affirmed. While Judge Sotomayor has commented on the impact of gender and personal experiences on judging, these two cases may suggest to some that such factors are unlikely to overwhelm her adherence to precedent and established legal standards.[29] The Second Circuit's decision in *Zheng*, moreover, may arguably illustrate an intent to seek clarification of the appropriate standard when it is unclear. Nevertheless, Judge Sotomayor 's comments and the absence of substantive opinions of abortion, as well as distinctions between the perceived roles of the courts of appeal and the Supreme Court, are likely to result in a continued examination of Judge Sotomayor 's opinions during the confirmation process.

Author Contact Information

Jon O. Shimabukuro
Legislative Attorney
jshimabukuro@crs.loc.gov, 7-7990

End Notes

[1] Remarks on the Nomination of Sonia Sotomayor To Be a Supreme Court Associate Justice, Daily Comp. Pres. Doc. 200900402 (May 26, 2009).

[2] *See, e.g.*, Raymond Hernandez and David W. Chen, *Nominee's Links With Advocates Fuel Her Critics*, N.Y. Times, May 29, 2009, at A1.

[3] 304 F.3d 183 (2d Cir. 2002).

[4] The restriction on federal funds to foreign nongovernmental organizations is referred to as the "Mexico City Policy" because it was first announced at a 1984 United Nations conference in Mexico City. Pursuant to the Mexico City Policy, foreign nongovernmental organizations that were interested in receiving U.S. government funds had to agree to a provision called the "standard clause" in family planning agreements and contracts with the United States Agency for International Development. The standard clause prohibited the organizations from engaging in activities that promoted abortion. In January 2009, President Barack Obama rescinded the Mexico City Policy. For additional information on the Mexico City Policy, see CRS Report RL3 3250, *International Population Assistance and Family Planning Programs: Issues for Congress*, by Luisa Blanchfield.

[5] 915 F.2d 59 (2d Cir. 1990).

[6] *Center for Reproductive Law and Policy*, 304 F.3d at 190.

[7] *Id.* at 194-95.

[8] *Id.* at 190.

[9] 494 F.3d 296 (2d Cir. 2007), *cert. denied*, 128 S.Ct. 2472 (2008).

[10] 467 U.S. 837 (1984).

[11] *Id.* at 843.

[12] *Shi Liang Lin*, 494 F.3d at 309.

[13] *Id.* at 327.

[14] *Id.* at 330-31.

[15] 497 F.3d 201 (2d Cir. 2007).

[16] *Id.* at 202.

[17] *Id.*

[18] *Id.*

[19] *Id.* at 203-4. Although the BIA acknowledged that a number of circuit courts of appeals had suggested that nonviolent, involuntary IUD insertions might constitute persecution, it nevertheless concluded in *Zheng* that involuntary insertion did not constitute persecution.

[20] *See Yahong Zheng v. Gonzales*, 409 F.3d 804 (7th Cir. 2005).

[21] *See Zheng*, 497 F.3d at 203 ("The BIA's opinion in Zheng's case was non-precedential and was signed by a single member of the Board.").

[22] *Id.* See also *Jiang v. Bureau of Citizenship and Immigration Services*, 520 F.3d 132 (2d Cir. 2008) (remanding BIA order denying application for asylum to allow BIA to articulate a consistent position on whether and under what conditions involuntary insertion of an IUD constitutes persecution).

[23] 361 F.3d 113 (2d Cir. 2004). Summary judgment allows for the expeditious disposition of a claim when there is no dispute as to either the material facts or the inferences to be drawn from undisputed facts, or if only a question of law is involved. See also Fed. R. Civ. P. 56 ("Summary Judgment").

[24] The Second Circuit also concluded that there were issues of material fact with regard to whether the Town's police officers used excessive force when they removed the plaintiffs from the demonstrations. See *Amnesty America*, 361 F.3d at 124 ("It is entirely possible that a reasonable jury would find, as the district court intimated, that the police officers' use of force was objectively reasonable given the circumstances and the plaintiffs' resistance techniques.").

[25] *Amnesty America*, 361 F.3d at 128.

[26] *Id.*

[27] *Id.* at 129.
[28] *Id.* at 130.
[29] See Sonia Sotomayor, *A Latina Judge's Voice*, 13 Berkeley La Raza L.J. 87, 92 (2002) ("Whether born from experience or inherent physiological or cultural differences, a possibility that I abhor less or discount less than my colleague Judge Cedarbaum, our gender and national origins may and will make a difference in our judging.").

CHAPTER SOURCES

The following chapters have been previously published:

Chapter 1 – This is an edited, excerpted and augmented edition of a United States Congressional Research Service publication, Report Order Code R40640, dated June 23, 2009.

Chapter 2 – This is an edited, excerpted and augmented edition of a United States Congressional Research Service publication, Report Order Code R40649, dated June 19, 2009.

Chapter 3 – This is an edited, excerpted and augmented edition of a United States Congressional Research Service publication, Report Order Code R40694, dated July 7, 2009.

INDEX

9

9/11, 50

A

abortion, ix, xi, 42, 43, 44, 45, 85, 93, 94, 95, 96, 97, 98, 99, 100
academic difficulties, 35
academic success, 6, 38
accommodation, 3, 5, 6, 7, 8, 10, 26, 37
ADA, ix, 1, 2, 3, 4, 5, 6, 7, 8, 9, 10, 14, 15, 17, 37, 38, 84
ADA Amendments Act, ix, 1, 2, 3, 4, 5, 6, 15, 38, 84
ADA Restoration Act, 15
administration, 26, 33, 75, 99
administrative, 12, 36, 48, 69, 81
advocacy, x, xi, 2, 10, 63, 94
Afghanistan, 83
age, 25, 29, 36, 37
Age Discrimination in Employment Act, 26, 36
agent, 46
Al Qaeda, 31
alternative, 5, 6, 30, 31, 38, 76
alters, 42, 95
ambiguity, 85
amendments, 11, 41
Americans with Disabilities Act, ix, 1, 2, 3, 14, 17, 37, 84
Antiterrorism and Effective Death Penalty Act, 56
antitrust, 67, 68, 89
APA, 86
appellate courts, 76
application, x, 3, 7, 9, 20, 21, 23, 25, 29, 30, 38, 40, 45, 46, 52, 56, 58, 60, 65, 97, 100
argument, 47, 66, 68, 69, 72
Arizona, 50, 51
arrest, 51, 52, 53, 55, 80, 98
assets, 75
asylum, xi, 42, 43, 44, 45, 93, 94, 95, 96, 97, 98, 100
attacks, 31, 50
attitudes, 23, 27
Attorney General, 65, 89
authority, 10, 11, 12, 31, 38, 62, 69, 80, 82, 83
availability, 42, 94
awareness, 11

B

back, 7
baggage, 31
Barack Obama, 85, 100
bargaining, 67, 68, 89
Bartlett v. New York State Board of Bar Examiners, ix, 1, 2, 14, 38, 85

beating, 55
behavior, 24, 35, 88
beliefs, 27
benchmark, 69
benefits, 8, 9
bias, 32
Bill of Rights, 11
bipolar disorder, 7
birth, 45, 97
blog, 80
bounds, 23
brokerage, 71
Bush administration, 26
Bush, President George W., 80
buyer, 71, 73

C

Canada, 32, 65, 66, 89
cardinal principle, 36
caretaker, 9
case law, 4, 12, 23, 39, 42, 60, 62, 95
cast, 31, 65
categorization, x, 19, 20
causal relationship, 99
causation, 70
censorship, 22
certification, 23
channels, 29, 30, 31
Chevron, 43, 96
Chief Justice, 76, 91
child pornography, 30, 31, 51, 82
children, 11, 13, 16, 35, 37, 38, 60
China, 43, 95
cigarettes, 59, 65
citizens, 33, 63, 64, 82
civil rights, ix, 1, 2, 3, 11, 15, 32, 34, 35, 37
Civil Rights, vii, 1, 8, 15, 32, 33, 37, 83, 84
Civil War, 29
classes, 32
classification, 33
classroom, 35
Clayton Act, 89
Clean Water Act, 68
clients, 73
climate change, 69, 70
CO2, 69
Coast Guard, 50
cocaine, 51, 52
collective bargaining, 67, 68, 89
Columbia, 2, 7, 10, 14, 27, 38, 81, 84, 85
Columbia University, 2, 10, 38, 84
commerce, 7, 29, 30, 31, 82
Commerce Clause, 29, 30, 31
common law, 65, 66, 69, 70
communication, 46
community, 11, 24
compensation, 7
competence, 27
competition, 89
complexity, 76
conception, 29
conditioning, 42, 94
confidence, 73
conflict, 31, 65
Congress, 3, 5, 6, 16, 21, 32, 39, 40, 41, 43, 44, 45, 66, 68, 70, 71, 72, 75, 76, 82, 85, 90, 96, 97, 100
Connecticut, 10, 11, 14, 21, 29, 33, 38, 49, 55, 88, 89, 98
consensus, 81
consent, x, 19, 49, 61, 66
Constitution, xi, 15, 21, 42, 49, 64, 80, 82, 87, 93, 94, 95
construction, 4, 43, 44, 72, 95, 96, 97
continuity, 80
contractors, 76, 77, 91
contracts, 85, 100
control, 21, 29, 44, 45, 61, 97
conviction, 49, 57, 73, 82
cooling, 68
coping strategies, 5
corporations, 63, 64, 70
cost-benefit analysis, 68, 69
cost-effective, 68
costs, 16, 65, 68, 75, 91
counsel, 56, 57, 58
Court of Appeals, x, xi, 19, 20, 28, 29, 31, 32, 42, 67, 72, 76, 93

courts, 14, 21, 22, 26, 27, 29, 30, 41, 49, 51, 56, 57, 58, 59, 62, 63, 65, 69, 70, 71, 76, 77, 81, 82, 86, 90, 99, 100
crack, 52
creditors, 74
crime, 52
criminal justice, 48
cross-border, 59, 62
CRS, 14, 15, 16, 17, 81, 83, 84, 85, 100
Cuba, 82
cultural differences, 101
customers, 90

D

death penalty, 21
debates, 15, 84
decision making, 47
decisions, ix, x, 1, 2, 3, 4, 5, 6, 7, 8, 9, 10, 11, 12, 21, 22, 24, 26, 27, 28, 29, 35, 37, 38, 42, 45, 46, 56, 62, 67, 68, 77, 81, 82, 84, 95, 98
defendants, 48, 56, 63, 65, 69, 77
defense, 27, 56
deficiency, 99
definition, x, 2, 3, 4, 5, 6, 7, 27, 38, 43, 45, 63, 80, 95, 96, 97
delivery, 49, 61
denial, 6, 21, 36, 40, 44, 54, 57, 58, 59, 63, 96
Department of Education, 11, 12, 14, 85
Department of Justice, 26, 45, 46, 64, 81, 86
Department of State, 47
Department of the Interior, 46
Department of Transportation, 50
deprivation, 39, 54
detention, 32, 50
deterrence, 77
developmental disabilities, 11, 38
disabilities, ix, 1, 2, 3, 5, 9, 11, 12, 15, 16, 20, 37, 38
disability, ix, 1, 2, 3, 4, 5, 6, 7, 8, 9, 10, 12, 13, 15, 16, 37, 38, 83, 84
disabled, 7, 8, 15, 38, 84
discipline, 7, 25, 74, 84
disclosure, 11, 23, 32, 46, 47, 48
discretionary, 54
discrimination, 2, 3, 7, 8, 9, 10, 26, 32, 33, 34, 35, 36, 37, 38, 83, 84, 85
discriminatory, 16, 33, 34, 35, 57
dispatcher, 52
disposition, 100
disputes, 39, 40, 59, 66, 75, 81
dissenting opinion, 20, 21, 35, 48, 49, 53, 59, 60, 91
distribution, 74, 75
District of Columbia, 27, 81
diversity, 63
divorce, 12, 61
donations, 23
draft, 67
drugs, 49, 80
due process, 11, 13, 16, 39, 40, 77
Due Process Clause, 28
duties, 48, 61, 65
dyslexia, 2, 10, 38

E

Education, xi, 11, 12, 13, 14, 16, 35, 38, 80, 84, 85, 94
election, 39, 40, 41
electoral process, 40
elementary school, 35
e-mail, 80
emitters, 69
emotional, 11, 12, 38, 44, 54, 96
employee compensation, 7
employees, 7, 23, 24, 36, 37, 48, 53, 77, 84, 87, 91, 99
employers, 24, 50
employment, 3, 7, 8, 9, 23, 24, 33, 36, 37, 68, 81, 84
enemy combatan, 83
environment, 11, 34, 37, 80
environmental factors, 69
environmental impact, 68
environmentalists, 69
EPA, 68, 69
Equal Employment Opportunity Commission, 6, 8, 14, 15

Equal Protection Clause, 33
European Community, 65, 89
Executive Branch, 22, 66
exercise, 26, 27, 36, 58, 60
exposure, 91

F

failure, 34, 45, 57, 58, 63, 70, 77, 88, 97, 98
faith, 51, 52, 81
false statement, 74
family, ix, xi, 13, 22, 42, 55, 85, 93, 94, 100
family members, 55
family planning, ix, xi, 22, 42, 85, 93, 94, 100
FBI, 47, 51
FDIC, 77, 91
fear, 44, 96
Federal Bureau of Investigation, 45, 47, 86
federal courts, 21, 30, 56, 59, 63, 70
federal funds, 16, 85, 100
federal government, 28, 40, 42, 46, 77, 94
federal law, 58
federalism, 29
fees, 13, 16, 75, 76
feet, 55
felony, 39, 40, 41
Fifth Amendment, 77, 87, 91
film, 30
fire, 23, 24
firearms, 27, 81, 82
firms, 59, 64, 65
First Amendment, 21, 22, 23, 24, 25, 26, 28, 32, 39, 40, 42, 80, 81, 83, 84, 88, 94
fiscal policy, 91
flight, 32
flow, 80
focusing, 76
FOIA, 45, 46, 47, 86
food, 49
Football, 67
Ford, 26, 81
foreign language, 3, 10, 38
foreign nation, 65
foreign person, 63
foreign policy, 32, 60, 65, 67, 83
Forest Service, 81
forfeiture, 58
Fourteenth Amendment, 28, 33
Fourth Amendment, 21, 48, 49, 50, 51, 52, 53, 54, 55, 77, 83, 87, 88
fraud, 65, 66, 70, 71, 72, 73, 74
freedom, 21, 23, 25, 26, 27, 42, 49, 67, 94
Freedom of Information Act (FOIA), 45
funding, xi, 11, 26, 37, 42, 93, 94
funds, 10, 11, 22, 37, 42, 43, 73, 74, 85, 94, 95, 100

G

gas, 70
gender, 99, 101
Geneva, 83
Geneva Convention, 83
girls, 50, 82
global trade, 64
goals, 64, 77
government, 22, 23, 24, 26, 28, 31, 36, 40, 42, 43, 45, 46, 47, 48, 49, 50, 59, 60, 65, 66, 74, 76, 77, 80, 82, 83, 85, 94, 95, 100
government intervention, 66
grants, 11, 16, 63
greenhouse gas, 70
groups, 69, 89
Guantanamo Bay, 82
guardian, 12, 54
guidance, x, 2, 31, 32, 45, 90, 98
guidelines, 8
guilty, 57

H

habeas corpus, 56, 57, 82
handling, 58
harassment, 10, 34, 48
harm, 44, 80, 97
hearing, 9, 12, 13, 15, 26, 39, 54
heart, 77
heart attack, 77
high school, 67
hiring, 7, 26

Hispanic, 33, 34, 56
Hong Kong, 60, 61, 62, 63
hospital, 8, 9, 36, 54
hospitalization, 9, 54
hostility, 2, 10, 35, 37, 38
House, 15, 84
human rights, 11, 38
humiliation, 54
husband, 54

I

id, 6, 28, 30, 40, 41, 44, 45, 54, 82, 83, 85, 86, 87, 90, 97, 100
IDEA, ix, 1, 2, 11, 12, 13, 16, 37, 38, 84
identity, 48, 72
ideology, 22
Illinois, 27, 28, 81, 82, 88
images, 52
immigration, 32, 43, 45, 69, 95, 97
immunity, 53, 54, 55, 74, 80
inclusion, 54
independence, 26
Indian, 46, 82
indication, 32, 90
Individuals with Disabilities Education Act, ix, 1, 2, 11, 16, 37, 84
industry, 7, 68, 82
inferences, 100
informational access, 12
inherited, 29
injunction, 12, 50, 69
injuries, 54, 98
injury, 7, 8, 44, 82, 97
inmates, 26
insertion, 45, 86, 97, 100
insight, 26, 33, 34
inspection, 46
institutions, 81
integrity, 74
interactions, 42, 94
international relations, 64
interstate, 29, 30, 55, 82
intervention, 39, 40, 66, 67
intrastate, 29, 82
Investigations, 46
investigative, 48
investment, 71, 75, 76
investment bank, 71
investors, 70, 74
IRS, 46, 47, 86
itemized deductions, 75

J

job performance, 7
job training, 7
joining, 40
judge, ix, x, 19, 20, 21, 22, 28, 31, 32, 33, 34, 35, 36, 41, 45, 51, 56, 57, 80, 83, 88, 97
judges, 20, 21, 23, 28, 33, 35, 52, 56, 63, 64
judgment, 8, 9, 13, 21, 34, 35, 50, 59, 65, 66, 72, 74, 81, 89, 98, 99, 100
judicial branch, 53
judiciary, 66, 67
Judiciary, 15
Jun, 82
jurisdiction, 12, 43, 59, 60, 63, 64, 95
jurisdictions, 62, 63
jurors, 56, 57, 80
jury, 8, 34, 35, 56, 74, 80, 98, 100
justice, x, 20, 21, 31, 48, 53, 83
Justice Department, 63
Juvenile Justice and Delinquency Prevention Act, 81

K

K-12, 38
Kennedy, John F., 32
killing, 44, 97
kindergarten, 35
King, 28, 82

L

labor, 67, 68, 89
language, x, 1, 2, 3, 4, 10, 11, 21, 38, 41, 44, 68, 71, 72, 76, 80, 85, 90, 96

law, 4, 12, 16, 21, 23, 27, 28, 29, 30, 33, 34, 38, 39, 40, 41, 42, 43, 46, 48, 50, 56, 58, 60, 62, 63, 64, 65, 66, 68, 69, 70, 71, 80, 81, 82, 83, 88, 95, 100
law enforcement, 46, 50, 65
lawsuits, 37, 72
learning, 4, 5, 15, 38, 52, 84
learning disabilities, 5, 38
legislation, 50
lenses, 4
liberty, 29, 54, 81
limitations, 9, 10, 28, 36, 38, 40, 71
liquor, 65
litigation, 46, 60, 66, 67, 70, 71
living arrangements, 62
local government, 9, 28
location, 60
long-distance, 7

M

mainstream, 29, 38
males, 82
malicious, 84
management, 35
mandatory retirement, 36
manipulation, 72
Maritime Transportation Security Act, 87
market, 67, 73, 74
marriage, 45, 97
Maryland, 22
meanings, 76
measures, 4, 5, 6, 15, 50
medication, 15
medications, 6
membership, 52
mental illness, 10, 37
mental impairment, 4
Mexico, 22, 42, 43, 85, 94, 95, 100
Mexico City, 22, 42, 43, 85, 94, 95, 100
military tribunals, 83
minority, 33, 59
minors, 29
Miranda warning, 87
misappropriation, 73
missions, 69, 70
money, 73, 74
motion, 10, 21, 74
motivation, 9, 33
movement, 49
municipal liability, xi, 93, 94, 98, 99

N

narcotic, 57
nation, 21, 64, 65, 68
National Football League, 67
national origin, 33, 101
national security, 22, 23, 31, 32, 50, 83
National Security Letter, 32
natural, 12
NCLB, 84
Nebraska, 22
neglect, 10, 11, 38
negligence, 99
network, 30
New Jersey, 87
New York, 1, 2, 4, 9, 14, 15, 20, 21, 23, 24, 28, 32, 38, 39, 40, 41, 49, 50, 52, 54, 55, 61, 69, 70, 74, 84, 85, 88
New York Stock Exchange, 74
New York Times, 84
NFL, 67, 68
No Child Left Behind, 84
non-citizens, 82
nongovernmental organization, 42, 43, 85, 94, 95, 100
normal, 5, 50, 88
nurse, 8, 36
NYSE, 74

O

obligations, 33, 57
Office of Justice Programs, 81
Ohio, 87
omission, 53, 71
operator, 54
oral, 32, 69, 83
oversight, 32, 74

overtime, 54

P

PAIMI, ix, 1, 2, 10, 11, 37
pain, 45, 97, 98
parenthood, 45, 97
parents, 12, 14, 16, 59, 61
parole, 40
patients, 10
PATRIOT Act, 22, 32, 66
peer review, 10
Pell v. Columbia University, 2, 10, 38, 84
penalty, 21, 75
pension, 8
performers, 73
permit, 13, 40, 67, 68
philosophy, ix, x, 19, 20, 31, 39, 75
phone, 29, 51, 80
physiological, 101
planning, ix, xi, 22, 42, 85, 93, 94, 100
plants, 68
plastic, 52
play, 67
plea agreement, 58
plurality, 80, 83
police, 9, 23, 34, 48, 49, 51, 52, 53, 54, 55, 98, 99, 100
poor, 73
population, 5, 44, 97
pornography, 30, 31, 52, 82
posture, 21
power, 29, 32, 61, 68, 74, 82
power plants, 68
powers, 60, 65, 66
precedent, xi, 14, 20, 21, 22, 23, 28, 30, 31, 37, 39, 42, 45, 48, 50, 51, 53, 54, 55, 56, 57, 58, 59, 60, 62, 67, 80, 87, 88, 94, 99
preference, 25, 27, 39
pregnancy, 43, 44, 95, 96, 97
prejudice, 58, 59, 88
President Bush, 25
press, 21, 22, 80
prisoners, 25, 26
privacy, 45, 46, 47, 48, 49, 50, 51
private, 3, 12, 13, 20, 24, 26, 37, 47, 69, 71, 72, 77, 87
probable cause, 49, 50, 51, 52, 54, 55
probation, 34
probc, 47
production, 31
progeny, 31
program, 10, 11, 37, 44, 97, 99
pro-life, 98, 99
property, 54, 75, 76, 82
propriety, 32
prosecutor, ix, x, 19, 20, 57
prosthetics, 15
protection, x, xi, 2, 3, 10, 33, 37, 42, 44, 47, 49, 57, 61, 81, 85, 87, 93, 94, 96, 97
public, ix, 3, 9, 11, 13, 16, 23, 24, 26, 37, 47, 69, 87
public education, 11, 37
public funding, 26
public interest, 47
public safety, 87
public service, 3, 37
Puerto Rican, xi, 94
punishment, 77

Q

qualifications, 40, 41
questioning, 83, 87

R

race, 24, 33, 34, 35, 36, 40, 85, 88
range, 21, 58
reading, 5, 6, 15, 41, 57, 59, 72, 76, 84
reading disability, 5
reasoning, x, 2, 3, 4, 11, 30, 34, 38, 55, 62, 75, 76, 82
recognition, 56
Reform Act, 70, 72, 81
refugees, 43, 95
regulation, 29, 30, 40
regulations, x, 2, 3, 6, 12, 15, 26, 38, 69, 73
Rehabilitation Act, ix, 1, 2, 10, 37, 84
reimbursement, 13

rejection, 6, 33, 34
relationship, 13, 23, 30, 50, 64, 73, 82, 90, 99
relevance, 31
religion, 25, 26, 27, 33, 36
remission, 4
reservation, 55
resistance, 100
resolution, 22, 41, 67, 70
resources, 37, 81
responsibilities, 7
retail, 71
retaliation, 24, 34, 84
retention, 60
revenue, 59, 60, 65, 66
Reynolds, 65, 89
RICO, 59, 65, 66, 67
risk, 66, 80
rule of law, 80

S

sabotage, 34
Sarbanes-Oxley Act, 70, 75
school, 4, 9, 11, 12, 13, 16, 25, 30, 35, 38, 67, 80
school authority, 80
schooling, 12
search, 49, 50, 51, 52, 55
securities, 70, 71, 72, 73, 74, 90
Securities and Exchange Commission (SEC), 70, 72, 74
Securities Exchange Act, 70, 71
security, 22, 23, 24, 31, 32, 50, 70, 73, 74, 83
seizure, 9, 49, 50, 51, 54
seller, 71, 72, 73
Senate, x, 19, 21
sentencing, 57
separation, 60, 65, 66
separation of powers, 60, 65, 66
series, 4, 13, 61
services, 3, 9, 13, 37
sex, 29, 33, 34, 35
sexual abuse, 54
sexual activity, 29
sexual harassment, 34
sexually abused, 53
Shell, 41, 90
short-term, 8
signaling, 77
signals, 60
Sixth Amendment, 56, 57, 58, 88
skills, 5, 6
smuggling, 59
Social Security, 8
sovereignty, 64, 65, 66
special education, 12, 13
specter, 83
spectrum, x, 19
speech, 21, 22, 23, 24, 25, 42, 80, 94
sports, 67
spouse, 44, 96, 97
St. Louis, 86
standards, xi, 23, 27, 36, 42, 70, 71, 94, 99
State Department, 50, 63
statute of limitations, 9, 36, 38
statutes, 10, 35, 37, 38, 41, 64, 65, 69, 70, 89
statutory, x, 1, 2, 3, 4, 8, 11, 21, 28, 38, 39, 41, 53, 64, 67, 70, 72, 76, 85, 89, 90
sterilization, 43, 44, 45, 95, 96, 97
stock price, 72
strategies, 5
strikes, 56
students, 25, 35, 80
subjective, 27, 75
supervision, 98
supervisor, 34
suppression, 22
surgery, 7
sympathy, 37
syndrome, 54
Syria, 32

T

Taliban, 31
taxation, 75
taxes, 59, 65
telecommunications, 3
telephone, 29, 30
tenure, x, xi, 19, 20, 31, 39, 42, 49, 56, 93

terrorist, 31, 32, 50
terrorist attack, 31, 50
testimony, 5, 34, 54
Texas, 81
thinking, 15, 84
threat, 82
threatened, 43, 44, 96
threatening, 35
threatening behavior, 35
threshold, 3, 7
Title I, 3, 7, 9
Title II, 3, 9
Title III, 3
Title IV, 3
Title V, 3, 8, 33, 34, 35
tobacco, 55, 59, 65
torture, 83
Toyota, 3, 14
trade, 64, 73
trading, 73
tradition, 28
training, 5, 7, 99
transactions, 30, 71
transfer, 10, 32, 35
transparency, 45
transport, 62
transportation, 9, 31
travel time, 24
Treasury, 87
trial, 5, 8, 34, 35, 49, 56, 57, 58, 74, 80, 88
tribunals, 83
triggers, 8
trucks, 7
trust, 73, 75
tuition, 13

U

uniform, 70
Uniform Code of Military Justice, 83
United Kingdom, 63, 64
United Nations, 85, 100
United States, 27, 29, 30, 31, 32, 46, 49, 51, 52, 58, 62, 63, 64, 65, 66, 69, 72, 73, 82, 85, 86, 87, 88, 89, 90, 100, 103
United States Agency for International Development, 85, 100
unreasonable searches, 49, 50, 51

V

validity, 28, 40
vehicles, 50
verbal abuse, 34
Vermont, 11, 12, 14, 21, 50, 85, 88
vessels, 31, 50
victims, 37, 74
videotape, 30
vision, 6, 89
voice mail, 7
voting, 40, 41
Voting Rights Act, 39, 40, 41
VRA, 40, 41

W

war, 83
Washington Post, 47, 83, 86
water, 68
wear, 80
wire fraud, 65, 66
Wisconsin, 87
withdrawal, 68
witnesses, 5, 48
women, 44, 96
work environment, 34
workplace, 7, 34, 84
WorldCom, 74
writing, 15, 22, 24, 34, 36, 38, 45, 57, 67, 68, 76, 84, 97
wrongdoing, 74, 77, 91